A Baptist Journey

A Travel Guide to Baptist Historic and Mission Sites in the United States

By Tony Coursey

Illustrated by Karen Ku

Eutaw Place Baptist Church, now a Black Baptist congregation in inner-city Baltimore, Maryland, is the home church of Annie Armstrong, first president of the WMU.

Contents

A Baptist Journey

The Grand Heritage

BAPTISTS IN NORTH AMERICA trace their heritage to the day, 25 years after Columbus discovered "los Indios, " when Martin Luther posted his 95 Theses in opposition to the Church of Rome, and the Reformation was born. Among the English protesters and reformers were a group called the Puritans, who wanted to cleanse the new Church of England, and the Separatists, who felt the need to separate themselves from the established church in order to worship according to New Testament principles

In the New World, these two clashed. And from their fiery conflict came much of Baptists' traditions — and one of the United States' most hallowed principles: separation of church and state.

Baptists in America

ONE GROUP OF PURITANS, called Pilgrims, sought refuge from the Crown's persecutions in the newly discovered America. In 1620 they landed at Plymouth Rock. With this group later sojourned an English clergyman, Roger Williams, who had been exposed to Separatist thinking and the witness of Baptist dissenters. In his own spiritual pilgrimage, Williams developed convictions that eventually led to his banishment from Massachusetts — the Pilgrims, by establishing an offical church of the colony, were repeating the mistakes they experienced in England.

In bitter winter weather, Williams fled south and established Rhode Island, the first American colony with separation of church and state. By 1639, he had helped organize the first Baptist church in America.

Today, about one of ten people living in North America is Baptist. On the average, one of seventeen individuals is Southern Baptist.

In the United States, the Southern Baptist Convention numbers 14.7 million members in some 37,000 churches stretched across eight time zones of

the western hemisphere, from the Virgin Islands to
Western Samoa. Baptisms are held in ocean waters
south of the Tropic of Cancer and in frigid streams
north of the Arctic Circle. The Southern Baptist
Convention is recognized as the largest Protestant
denomination in the world.

"The Baptist denomination," observed W. O.

*The Home
Mission Board
first met in
Siloam Baptist
Church in
Marion, Alabama*

A Baptist Journey

Carver, missions professor at Southern Seminary, "was a direct product of the missionary interest. Until 1814, there was in the United States a Baptist people, but no denomination. . . ."

In a few areas churches had cooperated, the first association being composed of five Philadelphia churches in 1707. These helped support evangelists, missionaries to Indians and back-country areas, and over time worked with sea-farers and developed other specialized ministries — the earliest home missions endeavors.

The consciousness of a Macedonian call to promulgate the gospel overseas gave impetus to the first national convention of Baptists in America. The legendary missionaries, Luther Rice with Ann and Adoniram Judson, left their New England homes in 1812 bound for India as America's first foreign missionaries. By the time these Congregationalists reached their destination, they had adopted Baptistic views. While the Judsons remained in Asia, Rice returned to the States to solicit support for them as Baptist missionaries.

From Boston to Savannah, Rice challenged Baptist churches and missionary societies to large-scale cooperation. Meeting in Philadelphia in May 1814, delegates organized the General Missionary Convention of the Baptist Denomination in the United States of America for Foreign Missions. The Triennial Convention, so-called because it met every three years, expanded its work to include education, a publication society and the institution founded by Rice, now George Washington University (D.C.).

In 1832, the American Baptist Home Mission Society was founded as the national agency "to promote the preaching of the gospel." Its motto: "North America for Christ."

Diversity and Division

OPPOSITION AROSE TO THESE "new-fangled institutions," as one south Georgia association called them. Differences were not new to Baptists. Theological variances existed early. Some, such as the evangelistic warmth of the Separatists tempering the Calvinistic tenets and ecclesiastical discipline of the Particular-Regulars, welded into strengths. Other theological differences caused the creation of new church movements, such as the Adventists and Campbellites.

The first major controversy threatening the Baptist identity was the movement opposed to denominational missions. Disapproving Baptists believed instead that "human effort" was improper and unnecessary in God's plan of salvation. An Indiana association voted that foreign missions were "not agreeable to gospel order." A Georgia association described educated ministers as "designing characters" and "false teachers." Luther Rice was labeled a money-raising schemer with impure motives.

This movement, which also opposed Sunday Schools and tract societies, spread from Maryland to Missouri, where 40 percent of the Baptists by 1840 were anti-missionary. Missionary-minded Baptists remained in the majority, but their advance across America was greatly retarded, especially on the western frontier.

The dark cloud of slavery also hampered nineteenth century Baptists. When it appeared that the Baptist agencies, located in northern cities, avoided appointment of slave-holders as missionaries, southerners decided "to confer on the best means of promoting the Foreign Missions Cause, and other interests of the Baptist denomination in the South."

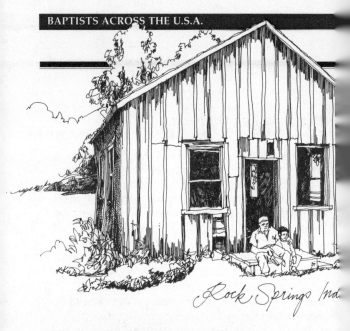

Rock Springs Ind.

The Southern Baptist Convention

ON MAY 8, 1845, IN AUGUSTA, GEORGIA, messengers created the Southern Baptist Convention, with the Foreign Mission Board and the Board of Domestic Missions. The convention also endorsed the independent American Indian Mission Association, established in 1842 by Isaac McCoy. Ten years later, the AIMA was absorbed into the domestic board, which became known as the Board of Domestic and Indian Missions — later the Home Mission Board.

Economics, lingering suspicions of denominational control, and other factors following the Civil War plagued Southern Baptists and their home mission efforts. Several Baptist state conventions turned to the better-financed American Home Mission Society, sustained by northern Baptists, which was eager to assist freedmen and expand throughout the South. The Board adopted a new image by moving to the resurging city of Atlanta and by appointing a new chief executive, Isaac Taylor Tichenor. His emphasis on cooperation and his vigorous leadership, which helped implement a sense of denominationalism among Southern Baptists, was only equaled by Baptist women. As early as 1808, Baptist women in the South had been

Century-old Rock Springs Baptist Church was an early work with Indians in Oklahoma.

organizing themselves into societies to support missions. South Carolina "low country" women first created the Wadamalaw and Edisto Female Mite Society. Soon many other Ladies Aid societies had developed, funding construction for church buildings, helping the needy, contributing to foreign and home mission causes — both by prayer and by offerings.

As these became numerous, committees developed to provide better cooperation and communication. In May 1888, during the Southern Baptist Convention (at which they were not allowed entrance), women constituted their own national organization, the Woman's Missionary Union.

The WMU saved the Convention from its financial struggles. Through its continued fundraising, promotion and education, women expanded the home mission witness in America.

Geographic Expansion

IN 1886, THE HOME MISSION BOARD started missions to Cuba, when many Americans expected the Pearl of the Antilles, so close to U.S. shores, to become another territory or state. In 1906, during the construction of the Panama Canal, the Board sent missionaries to the workers in the Canal Zone. Until recently, when the work was transferred to the Foreign Mission Board, the Home Board maintained work in both Cuba and Panama.

A Baptist Journey

Yet the Convention moved more hesitantly outside its traditional tier of southern states. Southerners who had migrated to Washington and Oregon formed in 1893 a Convention of the North Pacific Coast, which they hoped would be recognized by the Southern Baptist Convention. Distance and relations with northern Baptists kept the southern convention from ever recognizing messengers from the new convention.

In the Southwest, however, sentiments were so strong among New Mexico Baptists that southerners withdrew and formed their own state convention in 1910. In 1912, the two factions remerged, aligning with the Southern Baptist Convention. Similarly, Arizona Baptists organized a state convention in 1928 that won recognition from the SBC.

And as the Dust Bowl blew desperate Oklahomans and Texans to California, they took their southern culture with them. Forming the Southern Baptist General Convention of California in 1941, they too sought recognition from the SBC, which was achieved only after considerable debate.

Meeting in San Francisco in 1951, the Southern Baptist Convention put to rest its geographic self-restrictions. Having examined its territorial position, and with the Northern Baptist Convention changing its name to American Baptist Churches "so that it is continental in scope," the SBC resolved that "the Home Mission Board and all other Southern Baptist boards and agencies are free to serve as a source of blessing to any community or any people in the United States."

By 1963, often in response to requests from southerners who had moved into northern and western areas following World War II, Southern Baptists had work in all 50 states. "The northward movement of Southern Baptists," comments L.A. Loetscher, church history professor at Princeton Theological Seminary, "is one of the most significant religious phenomena of the century."

About this Travel Guide

GATHERED FOR MORE THAN A YEAR, material for this book produced a 600-page manuscript that has been culled to its present size — designed to be useful and managable: a wide cross section of Baptist historical sites printed in a shape appropriate for the glove compartment of a car, a woman's purse, a man's pocket.

We've tried to include practical information: phone numbers, hours of operation. We've tried not to send you 50 miles out of your way to a site that's now a cow pasture or an abandoned warehouse.

Nevertheless, the book is not complete, no more than Baptist history itself. If you find mistakes in the text or sites unworthy of a visit; if you have suggestions about places to include: let us know; we'll update subsequent editions.

WHATEVER . . . THE OVERARCHING THEME of this travelog you will find accurate and clear: that Baptists do have a grand heritage.

We have emphasized Southern Baptist history, but have not excluded any members of the Baptist family: for all contributed dedication and consistency, all faced danger and hardship, all suffered to create and to sustain the basics of our faith: freedom of religion, separation of church and state — respect for individual belief coupled with a zeal for missions and a devotion to starting churches and to ministering in Christ's name.

Baptists own a proud heritage, a grand tradition, carved out with sacrifice, love, courage and conviction, belonging to all, well worth remembering and cherishing, honoring and preserving.

To that goal this book is dedicated.

NEW ENGLAND

Baptist Roots in America

NEW ENGLAND IS BAPTISTS' HEART. HERE —
in Rhode Island — was started the first
Baptist church in America. From here
— in Kittery, Maine — came the group
who constituted what was to become the first
Southern Baptist church, First Baptist of Charleston, South Carolina.

This is the home of many early Southern Baptist
leaders. And the Baptist missionary movement has
its roots in New England's rocky soil.

Baptist heritage and tradition abound here.

In the early 1600s, about the time the Pilgrims
landed at Plymouth, the Baptist movement was
beginning in England. In 1631, Roger Williams, a
Cambridge graduate and Anglican ordinate
influenced by Baptistic teachings, moved to
Plymouth, Massachusetts, where his "strange
opinions" brought him into conflict with state-
church authorities. Ordered to cease preaching,
Williams fled, eventually finding in southern New
England a suitable place to settle, a haven for a
"lively experiment" in true religious freedom, a gift
of God — Providence. There, attesting his "Ana-
baptist" faith, Roger Williams was baptized.

In 1638 he helped found the first Baptist church
in America.

Rhode Island, the first American colony offering
separation of church and state, attracted other
settlers, among them Anne Hutchinson, one of the
first women preachers in America, and physician
John Clarke, who organized a congregation in
Newport and became an early leader of Baptists.

MEANWHILE, OTHER BAPTIST CHURCHES were forming.
First Baptist Church of Boston, which met secretly
for several years, ordained William Screven, who
soon was gathering Baptists for worship in his
home in Kittery, Maine (then part of Massachu-

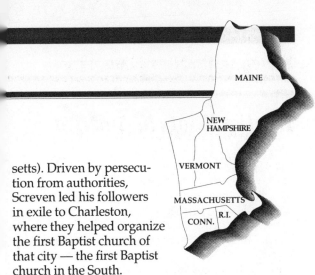

setts). Driven by persecution from authorities, Screven led his followers in exile to Charleston, where they helped organize the first Baptist church of that city — the first Baptist church in the South.

Among other events and people of New England were Mary Webb, who organized the first woman's missionary society in the world; and the first Baptist foreign missionaries from America. In 1812, Luther Rice and Adoniram and Ann Judson, all of Massachusetts, went as Congregational missionaries to India, but upon arriving there they became Baptist.

Rice returned to the U.S. to secure funds for the support of the Judsons. As a result of his efforts, Baptists nationwide organized for the first time into a convention, and began cooperating and working together for missions.

Through missions, Southern Baptists have come home again to New England.

In 1958, transplanted Southern Baptist military personnel — aided by the Home Mission Board — helped start Screven Memorial Baptist Church in Portsmouth, New Hampshire, the first church in New England established as Southern Baptist.

In 1963, an SBC church was constituted in Vermont, the 50th state in which Southern Baptists were represented. Today, with more than 70 Southern Baptist churches speaking a dozen languages, New England, the root of Baptist work in America, has become the symbol of Southern Baptists' expansion from a regional to a national convention.

Portsmouth, New Hampshire

Screven Memorial Church
397 LaFayette Road, near U.S. 1 By-Pass
Phone: 603/436-8623
Sunday Worship: 8:15 a.m. and 11 a.m.
Groups call ahead for tours.

AFTER THE 509TH BOMB WING was transferred from New Mexico to Pease Air Force Base, outside Portsmouth, in 1958, 44 people, many of them military personnel, gathered to form a Southern Baptist mission. Using Congregational church facilities, the Newington Southern Baptist Chapel was sponsored by South Hill Church in Roswell, New Mexico.

When the fledgling congregation appealed to the Home Mission Board for assistance, a home missionary, Gene Trawick, was appointed to serve as their first pastor, and their sponsorship was transferred to the "closest" Southern Baptist Church, Manhatten church in New York City. Two months later, on February 22, 1960, they were constituted into a church, the first SBC work in New England.

They chose their name in memory of William Screven, the Baptist pastor who lived across the river in Kittery *(opposite)*. Screven, the man, took Baptists south, and Screven, the church, returned Southern Baptists to their roots.

Kittery, Maine

MAINE

N.H.

Screven Homesite
Approx. 4 miles east on Rte. 103
on the west bank of Spruce Creek,
not far from Kittery Point
Baptist Church.

Kittery Point Baptist Church
Foyes Lane and Me. Rte. 103
Phone: 207/439-4077
Sunday Worship: 11 a.m.

IN 1673, WILLIAM SCREVEN, an English shipwright, and his wife, Bridget, moved to Maine,
a "haven of dissenters" from the official church
of the Massachusetts colony (of which Maine
was a part until 1820). A Baptist ordained in
Boston, Screven gathered others in his home, on the
west bank of Spruce Creek, for worship. He joined
local residents' appeal to the English Crown to take
direct control of Maine and establish religious
liberty. Called into court repeatedly for his "offen-
sive speeches concerning baptism," Screven eventually was coerced into fleeing the persecution he
found in Maine. By 1696, he and members of his
congregation had migrated to Charleston, South
Carolina, where they gathered as the first Baptist
church in the South.

Eventually, Baptists reappeared in Maine, and
the present Kittery church, today affiliated with the
American Baptists, traces its heritage to 1811.

Boston, Massachusetts

First Baptist Church
Early Site
Corner of Salem and Stillman Streets
(First Church presently worships at 110 Common-
wealth Avenue in the Back Bay area. The church is
worth visiting for its friezes of the sacraments, by
Statue of Liberty-sculptor Bartholdi, and its Tiffany-
designed stained glass windows. 617/267-3148)

Mary Webb Home
24-26 Hull Street
In front of Old North Church

WHILE NO BUILDING REMAINS, the site of the first meetinghouse of Boston Baptists merits a visit. Located in the North End, close to Old North Church and the Paul Revere house, the only reminder today is a street named for Samuel Stillman, during whose pastorate a second meeting house was constructed in 1771.

The first pastor was Thomas Gould (or Goold), a carriage maker who was suspended from the Congregational church for refusing to have his infant child baptized.

Gould organized the first Baptist church of Boston in his home in 1665, in defiance of Bay Colony law which solely recognized the Congregational church. In 1679, to escape notice of the authorities, the church built a two-story structure designed to resemble a private residence. Worshippers arrived one Sunday, however, to find the doors nailed shut by order of the General Court. The group worshipped outside in the cold March rain and expected to do so again the following week, but they found the doors mysteriously open. Never again did the civil authorities close the church.

Notable events occurring at First Church include the baptism of William Screven; establishment of the Massachusetts Baptist Missionary

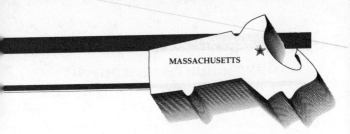

Society in 1802 — the first state-wide Baptist association and one of the first missionary societies in America; and organization of Newton Theological Institute, the first institution for training Baptist ministers.

NEARBY IS THE HOME OF MARY WEBB, a member of Second Church who in 1800 organized the Boston Female Society for Missionary Purposes, the first woman's missionary society in the world.

The society's appeals for other Baptist women across the nation to organize themselves began the movement for promotion and education of Baptist missions.

Museum of Afro-American History
8 Smith Court, off Joy Street
Phone: 617/742-1854
Hours: 10 a.m.—4 p.m., Tues.-Fri.

ON BEACON HILL STANDS one of the oldest Black church buildings in the nation. In 1805, several Blacks were baptized at First Church. The following year, Reverend Thomas Paul organized them and other free Blacks of Boston into the African Baptist Church Society, and built this brick structure. In its basement on the night of January 6, 1832, William Lloyd Garrison and 12 others organized the New England Anti-Slavery Society, reknown for its role in the emancipation movement and the Underground Railroad. Prominent abolitionists, including Fredrick Douglass, Wendell Phillips and Charles Sumner, spoke from the church's pulpit.

Peoples Baptist Church in Roxbury is direct successor to this early congregation.

Northborough, Massachusetts

Luther Rice Homesite

81 Lincoln Street, at the corner of Oak Avenue
Phone: 508/393-2404
Hours: None set; please call ahead.

B IRTHPLACE OF LUTHER RICE (1783-1836), one of
the first foreign missionaries from America
and pioneer of Baptist cooperation. On
February 6, 1812, as Rice, Adoniram
Judson, and others were being ordained, they were
joined by Adoniram's bride, Ann, who quietly
knelt with them. Her boldness spoke to her sense
of calling and dedication to the missionary task
before them.

Two weeks later, Rice and the Judsons embarked for India. During their journey Adoniram
became convinced of Baptist views while translating the New Testament Greek word, *baptizo*. Soon
after arrival, Ann concurred, later writing: "We are
confirmed Baptists not because we wanted to be
but because truth compelled us to be."

Their conversations with Rice led him to the
same decision, whereupon he returned home to
solicit financial support from Baptists.

At that time, Baptists sponsored no foreign missions nor any unified work. Rice's idea of a national convention led to the Triennial Convention,
organized May 1814.

He also encouraged formation of Baptist state
conventions and women's missionary societies,
and established the first Baptist newspaper. To
promote these causes and missions at home and
abroad, he travelled across the country, sometimes
riding as many as 93 miles a day on horseback or in
his carriage. He had no home and his clothes
became tattered, but he kept virtually nothing for
himself as he challenged others to contribute to
Baptist educational work and missions.

Purchased by the Home Mission Board in 1968,
the Rice Homesite has been renovated by volunteers into the Center for Missions and Training. The

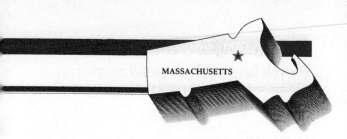

turn-of-the-century house, which stands on the stone foundation of the original Rice home, has been supplied with period furnishings through the generosity of an anonymous donor and Georgia Baptists. The blacksmith shop now houses a museum and guestrooms. The barn serves as a training center.

Rice Memorial Church

85 Lincoln Street
Phone: 508/393-3481
Sunday Worship: 11 a.m. and 6 p.m.

IN 1952, A FAMILY FROM WESTBORO, MASSACHUSETTS, became Baptists while visiting relatives in Florida. Eight years later, with a Baptist family from Northborough, and with Home Mission Board help, they organized into a church. Named in honor of Luther Rice, the church acquired its present site, part of the Rice Farm, in 1970. Here in 1983 messengers constituted the Baptist General Convention of New England and officially established the convention WMU.

Luther Rice House

Providence, Rhode Island

First Baptist Church
75 North Main Street, at Waterman Street
Phone: 401/751-2266
Sunday Worship: 10:30 a.m. (summer), 11 a.m. (winter)
Church tours: 9 a.m.—4 p.m. , April-October.

Roger Williams National Memorial Park
Visitor's Center at 282 North Main Street
Phone: 401/528-5385
Hours: 8 a.m.—4:30 p.m. weekdays.

ORGANIZED IN 1638 BY ROGER WILLIAMS, this is the first Baptist church in America. The present structure with its 185-foot tower was built in 1775. An inscription on the tower bell reflects an historic Baptist principle: "For freedom of conscience the town was first planted . . ."

This was also the site where southern and northern Baptists convened together as a single body for the final time. During the 1844 Triennial Convention, southerners walked out because slaveowners were not considered for missionary appointment. They formed their own convention in Augusta, Georgia, the following year.

NEARBY, THE ROGER WILLIAMS PARK celebrates the Baptist preacher who formed the colony where "no man should be molested for his conscience." The old homes, steep hills and narrow streets remind one of the area where Williams initiated the "lively experiment" in religious liberty, pioneering the way for future generations.

The Hahn Memorial marks the site of the spring used by the Williams family, whose house stood directly across the street. Originally buried next to his house, Williams remains are now entombed on Prospect Terrace, where a statue of him overlooks the city. Brown University *(on College Hill, behind First Church)* was the first Baptist institution of higher education in America. University Hall,

between Waterman and George Streets and near
Prospect Street, is the original edifice of the college
when it moved to this site in 1770.

United Baptist Clarke Memorial Church

30 Spring Street
Phone: 401/847-3210 (9 a.m.—noon weekdays)
Sunday Worship: 10:30 a.m.

U NITED CHURCH is the successor of the
original church founded by John Clarke,
a contemporary of Roger Williams. The
congregation, largely dissenters who
were banished or exiled from Massachusetts, migrated here with Clarke as he and William Cod-
dington founded Newport about 1639.

Not until the following decade did the church
become Baptist. Thus, while this congregation
likely pre-dates First Church in Providence, it is
regarded as the second Baptist church in America.

These early Baptists were influential in the
movement for religious liberty. In 1652, the church
baptized a slave named "Jack, a colored man,"
perhaps the first Black Baptist.

In 1663, Clarke who had been jailed once for his
beliefs, secured the charter from Charles II for the
colony of Rhode Island, with the terms that no person "at any time hereafter shall be in anywise molested, punished, disquieted or called in question
for differences in opinions in matters of religion."

A few blocks away from the church, adjacent to
a small park on West Broadway, is a private cemetery deeded to the church by Clarke. Through the
wrought-iron fence can be seen his grave and those
of two of his three wives and about a dozen other
early church members. A small plaque at the site
honors the pastor and town founder.

Suffield, Connecticut

CONNECTICUT

Village Center
Intersection of Rtes. 75 and 168

CLOSE TO THE CONNECTICUT RIVER and near the Massachusetts border lies Suffield, birthplace of Daniel Perrin Bestor (1897-1869), the first Corresponding Secretary (president) of the Home Mission Board.

Born February 2, 1797, Bestor was raised in a family who probably became Baptist as a result of the Great Awakening. His mother, Dorcas, was a constituting member of the Baptist Female Society of Second Church, established in 1805. His father, Daniel, was a deacon. Both parents and other family members are buried in the Old Center Cemetery, behind the First Church of Christ Congregational (on the west side of North Main Street).

Further down the hill, incidently, is Filer Brook, the closest "baptistry" to the church.

On the west side of town center is Suffield Academy, established in 1833 as the Connecticut Baptist Literary Institution. It had evolved from the local Baptist Education Society, organized in 1820 "to educate young men for the ministry."

When Bestor left Suffield in 1819, after completing his duty with the Connecticut Militia, he went to study law in Lexington, Kentucky. He became a state legislator in Alabama and Mississippi. His life, however, was intertwined with his denomination. In addition to being leader of the Home Mission Board, he was a theology instructor, president of the Mississippi Baptist Convention (1865), and a pastor the last ten years of his life (1859-69).

Other Points of Interest

BOSTON, MASSACHUSETTS
• **Tremont Temple Church** *(88 Tremont Street)*. The first free and integrated Baptist church in America, organized in 1839, "where every man, rich or poor, white or black should be on the same religious level." Dwight L. Moody described it as the "pulpit of America," having preached there along with other evangelists, such as Billy Graham, G. Campbell Morgan and Billy Sunday.
• **Old State House** *(corner of Washington and State Streets)* was site, in 1651, where Obadiah Holmes was publicly whipped for having preached against infant baptism. He fled to Newport, RI, where he joined the Baptist church of John Clarke. Again in Massachusetts, he was arrested for preaching Baptistic views, he was sentenced to pay heavy fines or be "well whipt." Friends offered the money. Holmes, however, refused and consequently bore 30 stripes that left him sore for weeks. Twice a pastor, he died in Newport in 1682, at age 76.

SALEM, MASSACHUSETTS
Tabernacle Congregational Church *(Washington and Federal Streets)*, where Rice and the Judsons were ordained, and Salem Derby Wharf (Maritime National Historic Park), where a memorial near the docking area commemorates the first American foreign missionaries.

NEWPORT, RHODE ISLAND
Seventh Day Baptist Meetinghouse *(The Newport Historical Society, 82 Truro Street)*. The historical society, with a fine collection of Sabbatarian records and other historical materials, occupies the meetinghouse of the Church, constituted 1671. Here the first known Indian Baptist, a Connecticut man named Japheth, was baptized in 1674.

ST. JOHNSBURY, VERMONT
South Congregational Church *(11 Main Street)* was the home church of Milo P. Jewett, renown Baptist educator and first recording secretary (president) of the Home Mission Board. Raised a Congregationalist, Jewett became a Baptist about 1838. He moved to Marion, Ala., where he founded a women's college and later assisted in the founding of the Home Board. His father, on reading a pamphlet on baptism by Milo, declared hotly, "I ought to have taught the boy better."

MID-ATLANTIC

Cradle of Home Missions

Today's SOUTHERN BAPTIST WORK in the Mid-Atlantic states has its roots in Maryland. The state was one of nine to form the Southern Baptist Convention in 1845, and a century later, when Southern Baptists were expanding beyond their traditional boundaries, Maryland Baptists were quick to sponsor missions in the District of Columbia, New England, New York and Pennsylvania.

That heritage of missions concern dates to 1836, when six Baptist churches withdrew from an anti-missionary meeting at Black Rock to organize themselves into a "missionary body"— the Maryland Baptist Union Association, forerunner of today's Maryland/Delaware convention.

By 1925, the convention was voting to split its $100,000 annual budget 50/50 between state expenditures and the Cooperative Program — a pioneering move, but not unusual for a state that produced Annie Armstrong, first leader of the Woman's Missionary Union and the "mother" of Baptist missions education and support.

BAPTISTS HAVE BEEN PRESENT in all Mid-Atlantic states for centuries. In West Virginia, the work dates to the 1700s, before the state itself was born. A notable example of the vigor of early Baptists in the region is Matthew Ellison, a 62-year-old preacher who was appointed in 1867 to work in West Virginia's

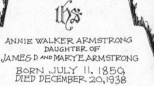

ANNIE WALKER ARMSTRONG
DAUGHTER OF
JAMES D. AND MARY E. ARMSTRONG
BORN JULY 11, 1850,
DIED DECEMBER 20, 1938

SHE HATH DONE WHAT SHE COULD
THE LORD KNOWETH THEM THAT ARE HIS

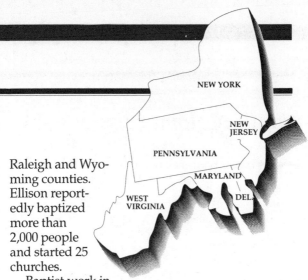

Raleigh and Wyoming counties. Ellison reportedly baptized more than 2,000 people and started 25 churches.

Baptist work in New York began even earlier: In 1657, two Dutch Reformed ministers reported that "last year a fomenter of evil came here . . . a cobbler from Rhode Island [who] stated that he was commissioned by Christ. He began to preach at Flushing, and then went with the people into the river and dipped them."

That cobbler — William Wickenden, pastor of Providence Church in Rhode Island — could hardly have imagined the Baptist witness that would exist three centuries later. Today in New York City, Southern Baptists alone report more than 160 congregatons, including language missions among Arabic, East-Indian, French/Creole, Japanese, Korean, Laotian, Mandarin/Cantonese, Polish, Portugese, Rumanian, Spanish, Tagalog, Ukranian and Vietnamese people.

All have developed since 1955, when Ohio Baptists organized New York State's first SBC church in Niagra.

SOUTHERN BAPTISTS MOVED into Pennsylvania about the same time, with missions planted simultaneously in the western, central and eastern parts of the state. By 1970, with support of Southern Baptists in Ohio and Maryland and guidance from the Home Mission Board, the work had become strong enough to form a state convention. Today more than 200 Southern Baptist churches comprise the Pennsylvania-South Jersey convention.

But Baptists' rich heritage in Pennsylvania predates the SBC's expansion in the 1950s. In the "City of Brotherly Love," Philidelphia, the first Baptist association in America was organized in 1707. Thirty- five years later Baptists adopted a statement of faith which did much to shape Baptist theology. Associational missions and chaplaincy were among early ministeries. Philadelphia Baptists established the first Baptist seafarers' ministry.

And the Triennial Convention, inspired by Luther Rice for the purpose of supporting worldwide missions, was organized in Philadelphia.

The other great Baptist tradition — freedom of religion — also finds root in the Mid-Atlantic region.

Baptist sentinels of religious liberty such as Isaac Backus and John Leland spoke to the Continental Congress meeting in Philadelphia, urging adoption of the First Amendment to the Constitution.

And soon after a federal city was established in 1801, six people gathered in the basement of the U.S. Treasury building for the first Baptist service in Washington, D.C. That was the beginning of the First Baptist Church, followed by many other Baptist institutions and agencies.

Today the D.C. Baptist Convention has more than 70 member churches, 40 of which are in Maryland and one in Virginia. Since Shiloh Church joined the convention in 1963, 16 other black congregations have been added, along with churches speaking Arabic, Portuguese, French, Spanish and Korean. Not only is there a high degree of respect for ethnic minorities, the convention is also sensitive to the rights of women. In 1964, it adopted bylaws which require one-third of the executive committee and all standing committees be laywomen. Thus D.C. Baptists continue to demonstrate the ideals of equality under God and freedom of religion that Baptists in the United States have held sacred for more than three centuries.

New York City

NEW YORK

Metropolitan New York Association
236 West 72nd Street
Phone: 212/787-7037

W HEN JAMES AARON of Illinois moved to New York City as a university student in 1956, he and his wife found no Southern Baptist church. By summer, they had located three dozen other Southern Baptists who together began worship services in the YMCA. Organized as Manhattan Baptist Chapel in 1957, it was the first new church begun in New York City in 40 years and became "mother church" of many SBC congregations in New York, New Jersey and New England.

By 1962, eight churches with nearly 1,300 members organized the New York Metropolitan Association. A decade later the association purchased this building, which today houses associational offices and three ethnic worship services.

The building also held the first offices of Southern Baptists' ministry to the United Nations *(now at 211 East 43rd Street, Suite 1201, 212/687-5150).*

Though the Manhattan Church dissolved in 1985, its influence continues as every new congregation emerges through these doors.

Metro Baptist Church
410 West 40th Street
Phone: 212/594-4464
Sunday Worship: 11 a.m.

O RGANIZED IN 1982 IN THE METRO association building, where it met for several years, Metro Church recently bought its own building close to the Port Authority, not far from Times Square. It is one of the few SBC churches in the city to occupy a church-type building. Since its inception, the multi-ethnic congregation has been active in a wide range of ministries.

Ephrata, Pennsylvania

Ephrata Cloister

*Pa. Rte. 272 (old U.S. 222), between Lancaster and
    the Pa. Tpke.*
Phone: 717/733-6600
*Hours: 9 a.m.—5 p.m. Monday-Saturday
    Noon—5 p.m. Sunday*

MANY OF THE 18TH-CENTURY BUILDINGS of a Baptist monastic movement survive and are operated as a historical museum. Under the leadership of Conrad Beissel, a German Pietist mystic, a group of Seventh Day Baptists settled here in 1735 under three orders: a married order of householders and a brotherhood and sisterhood of celibacy. The spartan simplicity of their lifestyles is reflected in the board benches and wooden "pillows" on which the sisters slept in their house, the Saron.

The celibate orders diminished by 1800, but those from the married order used the chapel as late as 1934.

Several buildings, including Beissel's log cabin, may be seen. The museum also sponsors *The Vorspiel*, a musical drama about the community.

Philadelphia

PENNSYLVANIA

Carpenter Hall
320 Chestnut Street
Phone: 215/925-0167
Hours: 10 a.m.—4 p.m. daily except Monday

IN THE NATIONAL HISTORIC PARK AREA a couple of blocks east of Independence Hall, the first Continental Congress assembled in September, 1774. An influential figure during their session was Isaac Backus (1724-1806), an itinerant Baptist preacher who along with other Baptists lobbied for a declaration of absolute religious liberty.

First Baptist Church
17th and Sansom Streets
Phone: 215/563-3853 (10 a.m.—2 p.m. weekdays)
Sunday Worship: 11 a.m.

FOUNDED IN DECEMBER, 1698, when nine people gathered in a storehouse near the banks of the Delaware River, the church built its first meetinghouse on Second Street. At that site, just north of historic Christ Church, the first Baptist association in America — the Philadelphia Association — was organized in 1707. Also there on May 18, 1814, delegates from 11 states constituted the first national body of Baptists, the General Missionary Convention of the Baptist Denomination in the United States of America for Foreign Missions (commonly called the Triennial Convention).

At the present site of the church is a Victorian building which dates from the era of George Boardman, an early Baptist leader and the step-son of Adoniram Judson.

Hopewell, New Jersey

Old School Baptist Meetinghouse
West Broad Street
Phone: 609/466-0103
Hours: 2—5 p.m., Mon., Wed., and Sat.

THE FIRST BAPTIST CHAPLAIN in the U.S. Army, John Gano (1727-1804), was born in Hopewell. His courage and close association with the Commander-in-Chief prompted Washington to comment, "Baptist chaplains were the most prominent and useful in the army." Gano, who later was an evangelist in the South and West, was ordained in this church. Also a deacon here about that same time, John Hart was the only Baptist signer of the Declaration of Independence. He is buried in the church cemetery.

For more information on Hart and the church, contact the Hopewell Museum *(28 E. Broad Street)*.

Madison Baptist Church
203 Green Avenue
Madison, New Jersey
Phone: 201/377-2121
Sunday Worship: 11 a.m.

ORGANIZED MAY 1, 1960, this is the first Southern Baptist church in the state. In its early years, it was aligned with the New York convention.

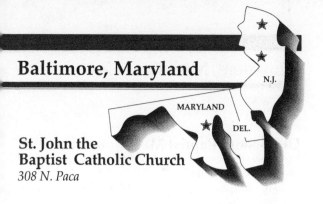

Baltimore, Maryland

St. John the Baptist Catholic Church
308 N. Paca

A FEW BLOCKS FROM ANNIE ARMSTRONG'S home-place and across the street from the Lexington Market (one of the oldest continuosly-operated covered markets) is the original 1847 building of Seventh Baptist Church whose first pastor, Richard Fuller, baptized Annie Walker Armstrong, at age 20, in 1870.

Soon Miss Annie began teaching Sunday School, regularly visited the sick, supplied food to the needy and taught a weekly Bible study at the Home of the Friendless, an orphanage then located close to the Lexington Market.

Armstrong House
1423 McCulloh Street
(Private Residence)

T HIS ROWHOUSE WAS THE HOME of Annie Armstrong, first corresponding secretary of the Woman's Missionary Union. In May, 1882, she organized the Woman's Baptist Home Mission Society of Maryland, the first Southern Baptist women's organization for home missions, with the objective to cooperate with the Home Mission Board. Twenty four years its leader, she dreamed that someday there would be a society in every church.

In 1895, as leader of the WMU, she helped start the Week of Prayer, Fasting and Self-Denial to benefit home missions. In 1934, the WMU honored her by renaming the offering as the Annie W. Armstrong Offering for Home Missions.

Baltimore, Maryland (continued)

City Temple
SE corner of Eutaw Place and Dolphin Street
Phone: 301/462-4800
Sunday Worship: 8 a.m. and 11 a.m.

A N ALL-BLACK CONGREGATION worships at the original site of Eutaw Place Baptist Church, where Annie Armstrong was a charter member. Edith Campbell Crane and Kathleen Mallory were also members while WMU executive secretaries. Miss Annie remained a life-long member, residing during her retirement years in the Cecil Apartments behind the church until her death in 1938.

Eutaw Place later relocated as Woodbrook Church *(25 Stevenson Lane)*. Its Eutaw Place Room contains Miss Annie's antique secretary (desk).

Greenmount Cemetery
Greenmount Avenue and Olive Street

H ERE ARE LOCATED THE GRAVES of Annie Walker Armstrong and Joshua and Eugene Levering, leaders in mission work in Maryland and the SBC. Miss Armstrong initiated the Christmas offering for foreign missions which honors missionary-to-China Lottie Moon. In turn, Miss Annie has become remembered by the Easter offering for home missions named in her honor.

Site of First Headquarters of Woman's Missionary Union, SBC
10 E. Fayette Street

O N THE SECOND FLOORD of this building was located the Maryland Missions Room, from which Baptist women published and mailed missions literature across the Convention. It also was the first headquarters of the WMU, as in-dicated by a marker at the site. *(Private residence.)*

Belle, West Virginia

Witcher Baptist Church

2206 East Dupont Avenue
Off I-77 approx. 10 miles
* south of Charleston*
Phone: 304/949-4587
Sunday Worship: 11 a.m. and 7 p.m.

EARLY CHURCHES OF THE AREA, dating from the mid-1700s and founded largely by settlers from Maryland and other coastal colonies, affiliated with the Baptist General Association of Virginia and, later, with the Southern Baptist Convention.

But after 1863, when the state of West Virginia formed and aligned with the Union, most Baptist churches joined the northern Baptists.

By 1868, 249 churches with nearly 15,000 members had withdrawn from the Virginia fellowship.

Churches that remained Southern Baptist did help plant other churches, and mission support was lent by Virginia, Kentucky and Ohio churches. By 1958, West Virginia had 33 Southern Baptist churches, most in the Kanawha Valley.

As Southern Baptists began stretching into the Northeast, they responded to requests from West Virginia Southern Baptists. Instrumental in rekindling SBC mission work was Witcher Church, begun in 1958 with the help of Ohio Baptists and the Home Mission Board.

In 1970, messengers from 52 churches assembled here to constitute the West Virginia Convention of Southern Baptists, the 33rd state convention.

Washington, D.C.

First Baptist Church
16th and O Streets, N.W.
Phone: 202/387-2206
Sunday Worship: 11 a.m.

I N THIS NEO-GOTHIC BUILDING eight blocks from the White House have worshipped at least two presidents, Harry Truman and Jimmy Carter. Carter also taught a Sunday School class. At this church was the first Sunday School in the city, originiated by Luther Rice, who worshipped here between 1813 and 1836.

National Baptist Memorial Church
1501 Columbia Road at 16th Street, N.W.
Phone: 202/265-1410
Sunday Worship: 11 a.m.

B APTISTS NORTH AND SOUTH worked together to erect this towering granite building as a memorial to religious liberty. It is designed with four main windows as Missionary Memorials. When the cornerstone was laid in 1922 by Charles Evans Hughes, U.S. Secretary of State and prominent Baptist layman, he declared that the contribution of religious liberty "is the glory of the Baptist heritage, more distinctive than any other characteristic of belief or practice."

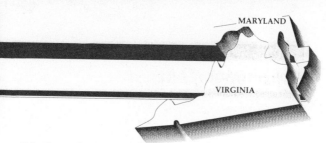

National Archives
Constitution Avenue, NW, between Seventh and Nineth Streets
Phone: 202/523-3000
Hours: 10 a.m.-5:30 p.m. weekdays

ON DISPLAY IS THE CONSTITUTION, with its Bill of Rights, which begins: "Congress shall make no law respecting an establishment of religion, or prohibiting the free exercise thereof." Much credit for religious liberty is due to Baptists, especially John Leland (1754-1841). When the original draft of the Constitution was sent to the colonies for ratification, Leland presented himself as a candidate to the Virginia constitutional convention, advocating more rights for personal freedom. His opponent, James Madison, favored the Constitution. At a meeting of the two men, Madison promised to support religious liberty in a Bill of Rights and Leland withdrew his candidacy.

Look also for the name of John Hart of New Jersey on the Declaration of Independence. He is the only Baptist among its signers.

Johenning Center
4025 Ninth Street, SE
Phone: 202/561-5200
Please phone ahead before visiting.

NAMED FOR MRS. ANNA BANKS JOHENNING, who attended the WMU Training School in Louisville and became a pioneer home missionary to the poor and underprivileged in the Capitol City, the present facilities were built in 1959 by the District convention and the Home Mission Board.

Other Sites of Interest

NEW CASTLE COUNTY, DELAWARE

Welsh Tract Church (*Glascow Road, 2 miles south of Newark, N.J.*) was founded by families who left Philadelphia Baptists after a dispute about "laying on of hands." They established in 1703 the first — and for nearly eight decades the only — Baptist church in Delaware. The present building was constructed in 1749, with bricks imported from England. Until about 1800, services were held in the Welsh language. While colonial General Baptists, like the early English Baptists, typically avoided congregational singing since it employed "hymns of human composure," the Welsh very much liked singing. In their Confession of 1716 they added an article, "We believe in singing the praise of God." This was the forerunner of the 1742 Philadelphia Confession. Thus, this congregation is credited with influencing Baptists throughout the Middle Colonies with singing, laying on hands and church covenants.

ANNAPOLIS, MARYLAND

Baptist Student Center (*201 Hanover Street*) meets in a 200-year-old house, one of only two in the city made of tabby construction; reconditioned by funds from Baptist Student Union Alumni to provide a worship and fellowship center for midshipmen from the United States Naval Academy and students at St. John's College.

BALTIMORE, MARYLAND

• **Westminster Presbyterian Church** (*Fayette and Green Streets*). Here on May 8, 1884, women from southern states met to have their own missionary meeting in conjunction with the annual session of the Southern Baptist Convention. The women decided to continue with their own annual meetings, which led to organization of the national WMU. No active congregation now, but the church still stands and its "catacombs" — burial tombs — are open daily.

• **Baltimore Harbor.** About 1892, Baptist pastor William Ritzmann of First German Church, along with his wife, began distributing literature to immigrants. About a year later, at the couple's request and with urging from Annie Armstrong, the Home Mission Board appointed Marie Buhlmaier to take up the work. Her sewing classes developed into the city's Baptist Good Will Centers. Today Kathleen Mallory Center (*1121 Riverside Avenue*) traces its ancestry to that work. Canton Center

(3202 Toone Street), organized in 1908, also continues a ministry to inner-city residents.

LUTHERVILLE, MARYLAND
Saters Church *(1200 Saters Lane)*, the state's oldest Baptist church, was organized in 1742 by Henry Sater, great-great-grandfather of Annie Armstrong. The original building, constructed from ballasts on English ships, is still in use today.

SILVER SPRING, MARYLAND
Korean Church of Washington *(310 Randolph Road)*, organized in 1956 by Changsoon Kim 30 years after he became a Baptist, is the first Korean Baptist church in America.

NEW YORK CITY
American Bible Society *(1865 Broadway)*, organized in 1816, today operates at an international level with offices throughout the world. Its board of managers and advisory council represents more than 50 denominations, including Southern Baptists. The society has contributed to the worldwide effort of translating the Bible in more than 1,800 languages and dialects. One of their most popular products has been the *Today's English Version,* prompted by a 1961 letter sent from Wendell Belew of the Home Mission Board. Belew described the need for a readable translation which could be understood by new readers or those adopting English as a second language. Robert Bratcher, a former Southern Baptist missionary to Brazil, undertook the project, whose success was far greater than the Society imagined. In 1974, Belew was honored with the 44 millionth copy of *Good News for Modern Man.* The New York headquarters, also known as the Bible House, has an exhibit gallery displaying historic Bibles, replicas of the Gutenberg Bible and Dead Sea Scrolls and other items.

WASHINGTON, D.C.
Nannie Helen Burroughs School *(5001 Grant Street, NE)* was named in honor of the Black Baptist woman who founded the school in 1909 to give Black young women "a fair chance to help overcome their handicaps of race." With advice and encouragement of her friend Annie Armstrong, Burroughs also helped organize a woman's missionary auxiliary to the National Baptist Convention.

THE SOUTH

Birthplace of Southern Baptists

BORN IN 1845 IN A DISPUTE with northern Baptists over appointment of a slaveholding missionary, the Southern Baptist Convention became the dominant denomination in the South. By the World War II era, when it began moving out of its traditional southern tier of states, it claimed about one in seven southerners.

But Baptist roots in the South pierce deeper than 1845.

Virginia Baptists set the standard for one of Baptists most important tenets: separation of church and state. The Virginia commonwealth had been decidedly Anglican since Jamestown was founded in 1607. There was no Baptist preaching until the end of the century. Baptists in England sent missionaries to Virginia in 1714, and early churches were founded in Isle of Wight and Prince George Counties. But they did not survive long.

Persecutions began as Baptists filtered into Virginia from the Middle Colonies and the Carolinas. Culpepper Jail was briefly home to several 18th century Baptists. Lewis Craig, after being jailed and harassed repeatedly for "preaching the gospel contrary to law," found relief by moving with his congregation to the western frontier. Not until 1787 was the law which established the Anglican state church repealed. By that time, despite fines and jail sentences, the Baptist population in Virginia had grown to be the largest of any state.

Persecution of Baptists was also severe in North Carolina. Had William Tryon, colonial governor from 1765 to 1771, had his way, there would be no Baptists. He described a portion of the province as being "full of quakers and anabaptists, the first no friend, and the latter an avowed enemy to the mother church."

THOUGH ANGLICANISM was the established religion for South Carolina as well, Baptists did not suffer

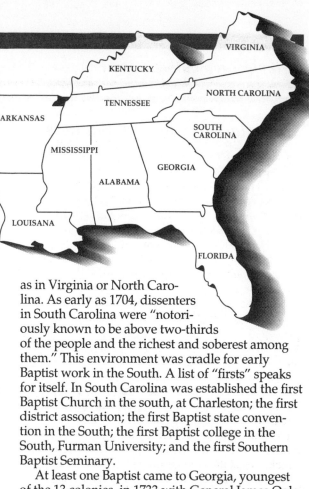

as in Virginia or North Carolina. As early as 1704, dissenters in South Carolina were "notoriously known to be above two-thirds of the people and the richest and soberest among them." This environment was cradle for early Baptist work in the South. A list of "firsts" speaks for itself. In South Carolina was established the first Baptist Church in the south, at Charleston; the first district association; the first Baptist state convention in the South; the first Baptist college in the South, Furman University; and the first Southern Baptist Seminary.

At least one Baptist came to Georgia, youngest of the 13 colonies, in 1733 with General James Oglethorpe. A handful of converts was baptized in Savannah, and a small number of congregations were organized up river. In 1758 a law proscribed worship "according to the Rites and Ceremonies of the Church of England." But Georgia Baptists sustained little opposition, and Baptist work there, as in the other southeastern colonies, grew rapidly.

LUTHER RICE, ARRIVING IN VIRGINIA in the early 1800s, was met by people who had great interest in planting churches. While riding in a stagecoach from Richmond to Petersburg, as he recorded, a "plan . . . suggested itself to my mind, that of forming one principal society in each state . . . [with] delegates to be appointed to form one general

Birthplace of Southern Baptists

society." Thus was born the idea for a national convention of Baptists, which was organized the next spring.

The Triennial Convention remained the unifying force in Baptist life until Virginia Baptists called for the consultative convention in Augusta in 1845.

The young Southern Baptist Convention, organized around foreign and home missions, struggled for survival. In Richmond, in 1888, as delegates debated support of missions, Baptist women — excluded from participating in the Convention — offered help by organizing an auxiliary agency, the Woman's Missionary Union.

Even before the SBC formed, Baptists were established in other southern and border states.

Prior to 1800, Mississippi was populated largely by Choctaw, Chickasaw, Natchez and Pascagoula Indians. Most White settlers were Roman Catholic. After the United States gained possession in 1798, there was rapid settlement by Baptists. The first Baptist church was organized in 1791 on Cole's Creek. The state association was organized in 1806.

At first a part of Mississippi Territory, Alabama was quickly settled after the Indian Treaty of 1807. A Flint River Association was organized with 176 churches in 1814.

The first all-Black Baptist congregation in America was in South Carolina.

SILVER BLUFF BAPTIST CHURCH

That same year George Gill, a Baptist preacher, settled on Arkansas' White River. Churches began to grow in number and the Arkansas Baptist Convention was organized in 1848.

Much of the population in early Kentucky came from Virginia and North Carolina, as did Baptist pastors. Squire Boone, Daniel's brother, preached at the fort in Boonesboro. He was the first Baptist preacher in Louisville and the first in the state to officiate a wedding service.

Kentucky's first Baptist church was organized in 1781 at Elizabethtown. The Southern Baptist Theological Seminary, organized in 1859 in Greenville, South Carolina, was moved to Louisville in the 1870s.

Tennessee Baptists had settled on the Clinch River by 1765, and two Baptist churches, probably started that year, were broken up in the Indian wars of 1774. Many early Baptists came from North Carolina, fleeing the oppression of Lord Tryon, the British governor. At Boone's Creek, one group in 1779 built the Buffalo Ridge Church, perhaps the state's first permanent Baptist church.

In 1821, the same year the United States bought Florida from Spain, the first Baptist church, Pigeon Creek Church near Callahan, was established. While a score of new communities were created during the territorial period and early statehood, the Seminole War (1835-42) and the Civil War caused disruptions. Many pioneer pastors left as fighting erupted with the Seminoles, who had resisted white encroachment and Indian removal to the West. Of the congregations which persisted, many worshippers toted guns with their Bibles to Sunday services.

LOUISIANA WAS THE NAME APPLIED to a vast territory west of the Mississippi River which extended from the Gulf of Mexico to Canada. The area was ruled alternately by France and Spain. Both of these

Birthplace of Southern Baptists

countries allowed only Catholic worship. Nevertheless, several Baptist groups tried to establish footholds as early as 1780. Baptist preacher Bailey Chaney was taken prisoner by the Catholic authorities, who turned him loose shortly thereafter but denied him the right to establish a church.

When the territory was bought by the United States from France in 1803, U.S. citizens began moving into the area rapidly. Soon Anglo residents replaced French and Spanish in the northern portion of state. The area became predominantly Baptist and remains so today.

In 1812, the first Baptist church, Half Moon Bluff church, was started.

Meanwhile, French people concentrated in South Louisiana where lived a mixture of original French settlers and "Cajuns" who had migrated to the area in 1755 from Acadian area of Canada (present day Nova Scotia). "Cajuns" is a corruption of "Acadians."

The Cajun people remained unpenetrated by the Baptist faith for more than 50 years after Louisiana became part of the United States. In 1870, Adolphe Stagg was converted to Christ. He became the first Louisiana Baptist missionary to the Cajun people.

In the Home Missions Room in Siloam church in Marion, Alabama.

Table of first HMB Meeting

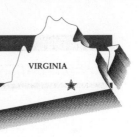
Crewe Baptist Church
U.S. 460 and Va. Rte. 49
Phone: 804/645-7464
Sunday Worship: 11 a.m. and 7:30 p.m.

Lottie Moon (1840-1912), missionary to China for nearly 40 years, stayed with her brother Isaac in Crewe during her last furlough in 1903. She attended Crewe church when not traveling — on one trip she asked: "Why send missionaries to Africa if you will not go into the miserable homes of our Colored brothers and sisters to uplift them?"

She was sincere that missions begin at home. During her "vacation," she and her sister-in-law visited Blacks, distributing food, clothing, instruction and compassion.

After Miss Moon returned to China, a terrible famine swept the country. Literally starving — she'd give her own food to others — she weighed only 50 pounds when she embarked for her journey "home" to Crewe. On Christmas Eve, she died while her ship was docked at Kobe Harbor. According to Japanese law, she was cremated. A highway marker at the town cemetery (not the church cemetery) indicates where her ashes are interred in her brother's lot. A Tiffany stained glass window of the Crewe Church is a memorial to her.

Miss Moon was born in Keene *(Va. Rte. 20, north of Carter's Bridge)* in "Viewmont," a home on the east side of the highway between Scottsville and Charlottesville. The original house burned in 1939, but its chimney bricks were used in the present house which is visible from the road. At Viewmont is a highway marker placed by the Virginia WMU to honor Miss Moon, whom Southern Baptists remember as the legendary missionary for whom is named the annual Christmas offering for foreign missions. *(Private residence; do not disturb.)*

Liberty, North Carolina

Sandy Creek Church
Sandy Creek Church Road,
*   North of Ramsuer and N.C. Rte. 49*
Sunday Worship: 11 a.m.

CONVERTED IN THE REVIVALS that swept New England, Shubal Stearns (1706-1771) with Daniel Marshall and others came south *(see also Appling, Georgia).* Hearing that North Carolina "was destitute," Stearns founded in 1755 the Sandy Creek Church, the first Separate Baptist church in the state.

In 1772, Baptist historian M. Edwards described Sandy Creek as "a mother church, nay a grand-mother, and a great-grandmother. All the Separate Baptists sprang hence: not only eastward towards the sea, but westward towards the great river Mississippi, but northward to Virginia and south-ward to South Carolina and Georgia."

After pastoring the church for 17 years, Stearns died. He is buried about two miles south of the church.

By the year of Stearns death, 42 churches had been started or become connected with the revival-ism that was born at Sandy Creek, and 125 minis-ters had been ordained and sent out from here.

The evangelistic impulse of Southern Baptists today is attributed to the Separate Baptist move-ment, and the pioneering spirit of men like Stearns.

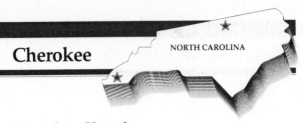

Cherokee

NORTH CAROLINA

Cherokee Church

U.S. 19 and U.S. 441
Phone: 704/497-2761
Sunday Worship: 11 a.m.

A T THE INTERSECTION IS A STONE CHURCH built in the 1920s with Home Mission Board funds, and for several decades pastored by home missionaries reaching out to the Cherokee Indians who remained in the area after the Indian Removal Act, when in the mid-1800s the U.S. Government transported the majority of Eastern Indians to Oklahoma Territory.

Cherokee Baptist churches in this area today can be traced to the work of Alred (Alford) Corn, a Cherokee who began preaching in 1840 throughout the Smoky Mountains. In 1858, the Domestic (Home) Mission Board appointed Corn a missionary, and with that financial support he was able to continue his work with the Cherokees who remained in the region after the bitter, deadly "Trail of Tears" march moved the majority westward.

Before the Removal Act, other Baptist missionaries had worked in this area.

One of the early churches was the Lufty Church, named for the Oconaluftee River, which later became the Mt. Zion Church, organized by Humphrey Posey. Its meeting house still stands in the Smokemont Campground, operated by the National Park *(10 miles north off U.S. 441)*.

Edisto Island, South Carolina

Townsend Tabby Ovens
Botany Bay (B.B.) Road, southeast of First Church off Rte. 174

First Baptist Church
S.C. Rte. 174 and Oak Island Road
Phone: 803/869-2662
Sunday Worship: 11 a.m.

THE SANDY LANE WITH ITS OVERHANGING TREES once led to Bleak Hall, the mistress of which was Hephzibah Jenkins Townsend. Captain Townsend, a deacon in the Presbyterian Church, differed from his wife on religion and other matters. At one point, she moved out of the big house, having smaller quarters and ovens built where the lane now ends.

The present house is near the ovens, on the tabby foundations of her home of exile.

From the river landing here, she departed every Sunday on a the six-hour canoe ride to attend the First Baptist Church of Charleston, 40 miles distant. From her pastor Richard Furman, she learned about Mary Webb and the Boston Women's Missionary Society. So she organized the women from neighboring islands into the Wadmalaw and Edisto Female Mite Society, the first woman's missionary society in the South.

To raise money for missions, they baked bread in these ovens, part of which remain extant, and sold the loaves on the highway and streets of Charleston. They also catered parties on the islands. From their profits, the women contributed money to Luther Rice for foreign missions, to the Charleston Association for work with the Catawba Indians, and to build the local Baptist meeting house on Jungle Road (*S.C. Rte. 174*), which still stands.

Mrs. Townsend was so loved by the slaves to whom she ministered, that she was buried among them in the church cemetery.

Beech Island

Silver Bluff Baptist Church

Rte. S-2-5, approx. 1 mile
south of S.C. 28 near Kimberly Clark
plant on the Savannah River,
south of Augusta, Georgia
Phone: 803/827-0706
Sunday Worship: 11 a.m.

THE FIRST ALL-BLACK BAPTIST CHURCH in America was not founded as such. In 1750, Thomas Galphin, an itinerate preacher and Indian trader, organized the Dead River Church at Silver Bluff, overlooking the Savannah River. Galphin allowed itinerant Black ministers, including "Brother Palmer" and George Liele *(see Savannah, Georgia)*, to preach. Many Blacks were baptized and admitted into membership of the church.

Consequently White members withdrew, by 1775 leaving the church to the Blacks who gathered under the leadership of David George and Jesse Galphin, both slaves on Thomas Galphin's plantation. Thus, Silver Bluff became the first Black congregation organized with Black pastors.

Operations of the church were disrupted when the British occupied Silver Bluff during the Revolutionary War, and colonists fled, taking their slaves. When the Blacks returned they found their meeting house destroyed. After meeting for nearly five decades in "goat houses," barns and brush arbors, the church built a meeting house at this site.

On the old sanctuary building, behind the new addition, is a marker giving the date of the original church (1750) as its year of establishment.

Charleston, South Carolina

First Baptist Church
61-63 Church Street
Phone: 803/722-3896
Sunday Worship: 11 a.m. and 7 p.m.

THIS IS THE OLDEST Baptist church in the South. The congregation first gathered in Kittery, Maine, in 1682 under the leadership of shipwright William Screven. The following decade, Screven and his church, persecuted by the established church, moved here and, joined by other Baptists who had migrated from England, re-established the church. Their first meeting house was constructed in 1699 at this spot.

William Screven and his followers lived close together in this immediate area, primarily near Church Street and Stoll's Alley.

The alley, named for Justinian Stoll, whose daughter, Catherine, married William Screven Jr., has some of the oldest houses in the city.

During those early years of Anglican-domination, the area was popularly called Baptist Town.

The house on the southeast corner was in later years the home of E. T. Winkler (1823-1883), when he was pastor of the church. Towards the other end of Church Street is Thomas Bee's House in which Richard Furman (1755-1825) lived during his last years as pastor.

Furman, who established the first children's missionary society in the South, was buried in the alley adjacent to the present church building, constructed shortly before he died. The 1822 structure, designed by Robert Mills, the architect who designed the Washington Monument (D.C.), contains several memorials to notable members and pastors. One of them commemorates Oliver Hart (1723-1795), under whose leadership was here organized in 1751 the Charleston Association, the first Baptist association in the South.

The church which has so many ties to notable

figures among Southern Baptists almost failed. Financially distressed after a cyclone in 1885 and an earthquake the following year, the church could afford no pastor and voted to close its doors in 1891. Determined women, however, climbed through the alley windows and continued regular services. They were joined by 60-year-old Rev. Lucius Cuthbert. With his help, the church officially reopened and continues today.

The Baptist Church at Beaufort
Charles Street, between King and Prince Streets
Phone: 803/524-3197
Sunday Worship: 11 a.m. and 7 p.m.

IN SOUTH CAROLINA'S SECOND OLDEST town is the birthplace and early pastorate of Richard Fuller, one of Southern Baptists' early eloquent preachers. Born in 1804 in Tabby Manse, a house (which still exists) overlooking the bay, Fuller was raised an Episcopalian though his parents had Baptist leanings. About the time he married, Fuller became a Baptist, and shortly thereafter he became pastor (1832-1847) of the church.

John A. Broadus, an early Baptist educator, wrote, "America has produced two great preachers, Jonathan Edwards and Richard Fuller."

Fuller preached the first annual sermon at the Southern Baptist Convention (1846) and twice served as president of the Southern Convention.

The present church building, on which construction began during Fuller's pastorate, was completed in 1850. It was used as a hospital by Union troops during the Civil War. The step-stones for carriages can still be seen in the left front yard.

Appling, Georgia

Kiokee Church

Ga. Rte. 304, between U.S. 221 and Ga. Rte. 104
Phone: 404/451-1086
Sunday Worship: 11 a.m. and 7 p.m.

A TALL MARBLE SHAFT in the middle of town indicates an early site of Kiokee Church, founded 1772. The oldest, but not quite the first, Baptist church in Georgia was also where the first Baptist association in the state was organized in 1784.

About four miles northeast of town is the present meeting site, near the Marshall homeplace. Daniel Marshall (1706-84), formerly a Separate Baptist missionary to the Mohawks along the Susquehanna River (Pennsylvania), founded the church and was first moderator of the Georgia Baptist Association.

Georgia was an English colony when Marshall and his wife, Martha, arrived in 1771. Marshall was soon arrested for openly preaching "contrary to the rites and ceremonies of the Church of England." Martha, "a lady of good sense, singular piety and surprising elocution," exhorted the arresting constable, Samuel Cartledge, to be saved from his sins. While Daniel was tried and ordered not to preach again, Martha made such an effective plea for religious liberty that Cartledge repented (later becoming a Baptist deacon and minister). Daniel was released and never harassed again.

As 18th-century Separate Baptist women preached, Martha became a popular speaker. An early report said: "In countless instances [she] melted a whole concourse into tears by her prayers and exhortations."

East of today's meetinghouse is the Marshall Historical Site, where the Marshall house stood. In the family graveyard their son, Rev. Abraham Marshall, is buried.

Augusta, Georgia

GEORGIA

First Baptist Church
(early site)

Southwest corner of Greene and Eighth Streets
Phone: 404/722-5571 (Dennis Caddell)
Hours: By appointment only.

BEGUN AS THE BAPTIST PRAYING SOCIETY in 1817, the church has contributed in various ways to missions. William Tryon, an early missionary to Texas, was licensed here in 1832. A few decades later the church started its own City Mission Board and Chinese Sunday School.

In 1892, Mary Emily Wright and other members of the Woman's Missionary Society produced the first missionary prayer calendar and offered it for sale throughout the Southern Baptist Convention.

But the most significant event here was the organization of the Southern Baptist Convention.

In 1845, the church hosted the convention called by Virginia Baptists "to confer on the best means of promoting the foreign mission cause and other interests of the Baptist denomination in the South." The church expected 130 delegates, but more than 300 arrived. On May 8, they constituted the Southern Baptist Convention with agencies for foreign and home missions.

Since, the Convention has expanded from two agencies to 20. Representing less than 400,000 members among 4,000 churches in its early years, the SBC now has 14.3 million members and 37,000 churches. Missions has remained a major thrust, with nearly 8,000 missionaries across the United States and in more than 120 other countries.

The SBC has become the largest Baptist body in the world and the largest non-Catholic denomination in the United States.

The present church structure of 1902, with its two Tiffany stained-glass windows, is being preserved by a non-profit foundation, Southern Baptist Birthplace, Inc. *(First Baptist Church now meets at the corner of Walton Way and Jackson Road.)*

Savannah, Georgia

GEORGIA

FLORIDA

First African Baptist Church
St. Julian Street at Franklin Square
Phone: 912/233-6597
Sunday Worship: 11:30 and 7 p.m.

ONE OF THE OLDEST Black Baptist congregations in America resulted from the work of George Leile (or Lisle), a Virginia slave whose owner freed him to preach. Leile preached on Savannah River plantations as early as 1773. Within the next four years he had gathered for worship the slaves of Jonathan Bryan, among them Andrew Bryan, baptized in 1781.

As Leile moved on, Bryan continued his work. Not allowed to have "big church" but every three months, Bryan gradually won the confidence of the White community and his freedom. Rev. Abraham Marshall (White) of Kiokee Church and Rev. Jesse Peters (Black) met with the congregation on Jan. 20, 1788, in a plantation barn to ordain Bryan and constitute the Ethiopian Church of Jesus Christ.

Despite harassment, Bryan secured title to land for the church. Following a rift, the majority of the congregation followed Bryan to this site and organized as the First African Church. The present structure, completed in 1859, was constructed by slaves as their masters allowed them the time. The stained glass windows commemorate early leaders.

First Bryan Baptist Church
575 West Bryan Street
Phone: 912/232-5526
Sunday Worship: 11 a.m.

When First African split, the minority remained at the original site, now the oldest parcel of land in the South continuously owned by Blacks and the oldest church property of any all-Black Baptist congregation. Chartered in 1867, the church has a memorial that pays tribute to George Leile, the first Black Baptist missionary.

Key West, Florida

First Baptist Church
524 Eason Street
Phone: 305/296-8544
Sunday Worship: 10:45 a.m. and 6 p.m.

CHARLES C. LEWIS, a Connecticut sea captain who had been converted in 1842, was in Key West a year later, going from house-to-house gathering a Baptist congregation. He was succeeded by G. G. Tripp, another American Baptist missionary who, in 1844, established the first Sunday School in Florida.

The church went pastorless for several years, before the Southern Baptist Home Mission Board provided a missionary, W. F. Wood, about 1883.

Among Wood's congregation were Cuban immigrants, whose personal testimonies made him aware of the need for the gospel on the island only a 90 miles to the south. As he walked through a cemetery one day, Wood was profoundly struck by the words on a Methodist minister's tombstone: "Don't give up Cuba."

Wood challenged Florida Baptists at their 1884 convention. They, in turn, brought the issue to the Southern Baptist Convention in 1885. Because the Foreign Mission Board had no plans to enter Cuba, and since some speculated Cuba might become part of the United States, the Convention assigned the work to the Home Mission Board.

In 1886, Alberto Diaz, a Havana preacher ordained by Wood, became first superintendent of Baptist work in Cuba, and for eight decades the Home Board supervised missions on the island.

Inside First Church's building, the pews are carved to reflect various periods or significant events in the church's history. Among the designs can be seen a geographic outline of Cuba, representing the work begun during Wood's pastorate, and the seal of the U.S. president, symbolizing visits of Harry Truman, one of two U.S. presidents who were Baptist, when he stayed in Key West.

Marion, Alabama

TENNESSEE

ALABAMA

Siloam Church
1003 Washington Street
Phone: 205/683-6313
Sunday Worship: 11 a.m.
Church open 8 a.m.—4 p.m. weekdays

PIONEER BAPTIST PREACHER Charles Crow helped found Siloam church about the same time the city was starting. Two decades after its organization in 1822, Siloam had become the largest Baptist church west of the Allegheny Mountains. The Alabama Baptist Convention met here in 1844, adopting the "Alabama Resolutions," which were precipitated by a split between northern and southern Baptists.

When the Southern Baptist Convention was established in Augusta, Georgia, the following spring, it selected Marion as the site for its Domestic (Home) Mission Board, which had its first organizational meeting in this church.

The church offered the basement "rent free" to the new agency, which remained here until relocating to Atlanta in 1882.

The church today has a Heritage Room, where may be found the table around which was held the first meeting of the Home Mission Board.

The present sanctuary is the third meeting house, dedicated in 1849. Originally located in what is now the western part of the Marion city cemetery, Siloam's first building was a simple log cabin. Its second, an elaborate frame structure erected 1837, was described as "one of the most elegant and tasty houses of worship in the state."

Early Baptist leader E. T. Winkler was pastor, 1872-83, and editor of *Alabama Baptist* newspaper, which had its offices in Marion for a while. He is the only pastor of Siloam buried in the local cemetery.

Prescott Memorial Church
499 Patterson Street
Phone: 901/327-8479
Sunday Worship: 10:35 a.m. (summer), 11 a.m. (winter)

EIGHT EDCADES AFTER ITS FOUNDING, Prescott Memorial — with 235 members — in 1987 became the largest Southern Baptist church to have a woman pastor. That wasn't the Memphis congregation's only first. In the late 1960s, it became the first SBC church in the area to integrate when a Nigerian college student, product of SBC foreign mission work, presented himself for membership. After a divisive debate, the church voted to receive him. During the next few years, Prescott lost more than 1,000 members.

In 1970, Prescott became the first SBC church in Memphis to ordain women deacons, a distinction it continues to hold.

When Nancy Hastings Sehested became pastor, she was one of 11 who pastor or co-pastor among the 450 Southern Baptist women ordained for the ministry.

The Shelby Association withdrew fellowship from the church in October 1987. Before the vote, messengers heard Ms. Sehested give this extemporaneous testimony: "You'll remember that Jesus was questioned about his biblical interpretation — in his own home town by his people, who wondered if he was reading scripture right by his interpretation of Isaiah 61. And you'll remember that they did not like his interpretation. . . .

"So I leave you with my testimony:

" 'The spirit of the Lord is upon me because God has anointed me to preach good news to the poor. God has sent me to proclaim release to the captives, and recovery of sight to the blind, to set at liberty those who are oppressed, to proclaim the acceptable year of the Lord.' "

Hodgenville, Kentucky

South Fork Baptist Church
About 5 miles south on Ky. Hgwy. 31E
Phone: 502/325-3626 or 325-3636
Sunday Worship: 11 a.m. and 7:30 p.m.

THE FOURTH BAPTIST CHURCH planted on Kentucky soil, South Fork was organized in 1782 under a large oak tree which served as a meeting place for the remainder of the summer. Immediately seven persons were baptized, probably the first such occurance in Kentucky. With hostile Indians in surrounding forests, armed citizens guarded the candidates to the water of Nolin River.

In the 1800s an anti-slavery faction of the church moved about three miles east of Hodgenville to organize Little Mount Baptist Church, to which Thomas and Nancy Hanks Lincoln belonged.

About three miles south of Hodgenville stands the Lincoln Birthplace Memorial, where Abraham Lincoln was born on February 12, 1809.

The present Hodgenville Baptist Church was organized in 1838. The Lincoln Memorial Baptist Church, located within a half mile of the Lincoln birthplace, was organized in 1949.

Louisville

KENTUCKY

Carver School of Missions and Social Work

The Southern Baptist Theological Seminary
2825 Lexington Road
Phone: 502/897-4605
Hours: 8:30 a.m—5 p.m. weekdays

IN 1907, ADJUNCT TO SOUTHERN BAPTISTS' first seminary, the Woman's Missionary Union established the WMU Training School, where Southern Baptist women could learn to teach the Bible and do missions (1907-57). Now that women have been incorporated into regular seminary classes, the Training School has become the Carver School of Missions and Social Work of Southern Baptist Seminary.

In 1913, the WMU Training School established a Good Will Center, where students could practice what they were learning. This became a model for similar centers, at first managed by WMUs throughout the convention, later moving under leadership of the Home Mission Board.

Agnes Osborne, corresponding secretary of Kentucky's Central Committee for woman's work, published in 1882 *The Heathen Helper*, the first woman's missionary periodical to be distributed Conventionwide. Osborne, a pioneer in social work, with the help of Louisville women, opened a mission at 1208 West Jefferson and was resident director until her death in 1930.

Neither the Good Will Center nor the mission on West Jefferson exist today.

"House Beautiful," the original Training School building, is now a United Way facility. It served the WMU from 1907 until 1941, when the Training School relocated on the campus of Southern Baptist Theological Seminary.

New Orleans, Louisiana

Baptist Centers

NEW ORLEANS IS A HISTORIC CENTER of Home Mission Board work. Among major emphasizes have been Christian ministries, most pioneering efforts, and many still in existence. The first Baptist rescue mission for women was started here, for example. Good Samaritan Home, established in 1953, provided emergency shelter for women with alcohol, drug, prostitution and other problems until it closed in 1969.

• **Rachel Sims Baptist Center**
729 Second Street
Phone: 504/891-2578
Established in 1919, this "riverfront ministry" began the Home Mission Board's good-will center work. Today Southern Baptists sponsor more than 120 Baptist centers throughout U.S. cities.

• **Baptist Friendship House**
813 Elysian Fields Avenue
Phone: 504/949-4469
Another early center, it now ministers on the edge of New Orleans' Vieux Carre (old city) district. As with all centers, it is staffed by home missionaries.

• **Carver Baptist Center**
3701 Annunciation Street
Phone: 504/897-2434
Named for George Washington Carver, the center ministers in a Black, low-income neighborhood.

• **Sellers Baptist Home and Adoption Center**
2010 Penniston Street
Phone: 504/895-2088
Founded in the 1920s as the Baptist Woman's Emergency Home, it originally provided temporary lodging for transients. By the mid-1930s the home had begun caring for unwed mothers. In 1944, it focused its entire ministry on pregnant women. Named for Thomas Sellers, an obstetrician who donated his services for 33 years, Sellers is the only maternity home operated by a Southern Baptist Convention agency.

■ *Please call before visiting any center.*

LOUISIANA

Clovis Brantley Center
201 Magazine Street
Phone: 504/523-5761

SINCE ITS FOUNDING as the Baptist Rescue Mission in 1927, the center has offered food and shelter to homeless men daily in the name of Christ. Within five decades, more than a million men had passed through its doors, with more than 20,000 making professions of faith.

In addition to its daily food-and-shelter programs, the center, open 24 hours a day, now offers help to men with alcohol and drug problems.

The center was renamed in 1984 for Clovis Brantley, a missionary appointed in 1937 to serve Baptist Rescue Mission. After two decades in New Orleans, Brantley came to the Home Mission Board in Atlanta, where he served for 20 more years.

During his career, Brantley helped initiate 118 Christian ministry programs and organize Baptist centers in 25 state conventions. He died in 1979, at age 66, with 40 years given to home missions.

First Baptist Church
4301 Saint Charles Avenue
Phone: 504/895-8632
Sunday Worship: 10:30 a.m. and 7 p.m.

THE FIRST BAPTIST CHURCH in New Orleans was established in 1843, under the ministry of Russell Holman, a Massachusetts native appointed by the American Baptists. Two years later, after formation of the Southern Baptist Convention, Holman accepted the position of Corresponding Secretary of the Southern Baptist Domestic (Home) Mission Board, becoming its second chief executive.

In its original mandate, the Board was instructed to witness to Blacks and to New Orleans, then the largest city south of Baltimore.

Other Sites of Interest

SOUTHERN BAPTIST AGENCIES
The five major Southern Baptist Convention agencies, all located in the South, welcome visitors. Open during standard working hours, all have historical displays and provide tours.

ATLANTA, GEORGIA
Home Mission Board
1350 Spring Street, NW
The Home Mission Board cooperates with churches, associations and state conventions to establish and develop congregations for witnessing and ministering. In addition to church loans and other field assistance, the Board has nearly 3,700 missionaries under joint appointment in all 50 states and American Samoa, Puerto Rico and the Virgin Islands. The Chaplaincy Division commissions some 1,200 military, hospital and institutional chaplains.

BIRMINGHAM, ALABAMA
Woman's Missionary Union
100 Missionary Ridge
Organized in 1888 as an auxiliary agency of the Southern Baptist Convention, the WMU provides programs, publications and promotion for missions education, mission action and mission support for 1.2 million women, girls and pre-schoolers. In 1984 it moved its national headquarters from downtown to New Hope Mountain, where its present home offers artifacts, archives and a library related to Baptist missions worldwide. Furnishings of several major rooms were provided by individual state WMUs and are called such names as the Georgia Lobby and the Mississippi Porch.

MEMPHIS, TENNESSEE
Brotherhood Commission
1548 Poplar Avenue

Founded as the Laymen's Missionary Movement in 1907, the Brotherhood has more than a million men and boys involved in missions education and missions action.

NASHVILLE, TENNESSEE
Sunday School Board
127 Ninth Avenue, North

The Sunday School Board had its beginning in 1873 as part of the Home Mission Board. Previously, Southern Baptists had been dependent upon the American Baptist Publication Society in Philadelphia for their literature. Today the SSB is the "largest religious publishing house in the world," turning out millions of pieces of literature for Southern Baptists' 37,000 churches. Next to the Board *(901 Commerce Street)* is the Historical Commission, where many Southern Baptist historical documents are stored.

RICHMOND, VIRGINIA
Foreign Mission Board
3806 Monument Avenue

After nearly 100 years in local churches and rented space, in 1935 the Foreign Mission Board moved into its own building at Sixth and Franklin Streets. In 1959, it occupied its present quarters, the center of Southern Baptists' worldwide missions efforts. The Board oversees the work of nearly 3,800 missionaries in more than 120 countries. Still officially known stateside as the Foreign Mission Board, the agency in 1987 approved for official use abroad a second name, The International Board of the Southern Baptist Convention. The FMB also operates a missionary orientation center in nearby Rockville, Virginia.

Other Sites of Interest

AUBURN, ALABAMA
Ebenezer Missionary Baptist Church *(on Baptist Hill, East Thach Avenue)*. Built before 1870 by newly freed Black men and women, it was restored in 1969-70 by the Auburn Heritage Association, after the congregation moved to a new building on Pitts Street.

MICANOPY, FLORIDA
First Baptist Church *(Fla. Rte. 234, between U.S. 441 and I-75)*. In 1881, A.B. Hester Bailey, wife of missionary pastor Napolean A. Bailey, with 15 other women organized a missionary society. That same year she was seated as a messenger to the Florida Convention, which appointed her its secretary for woman's work, for which she began receiving a small stipend from the Home Mission Board. Before her death in 1886, she helped secure the appointment of Miss Adela Falles as a missionary to the Cubans in Key West. In 1912, the Florida WMU erected a monument to her in the church cemetery.

ATLANTA, GEORGIA
King Center for Nonviolent Social Change *(449 Auburn Avenue, NE)*. National Historic District honors Martin Luther King Jr. (1929-68), champion of civil rights and the only Baptist ever to receive the Nobel Peace Prize. His birthplace *(503 Auburn)* and Ebenezer Baptist Church *(413 Auburn)* which he co-pastored with his father, are near King Center, which continues his work with conferences and studies for non-violent social change. The center also has an excellent museum and the slain leader's tomb.

SAVANNAH, GEORGIA
First Baptist Church *(223 Bull Street at Chippewa Square)*. On Franklin Square in 1800, Henry Holcombe established the first Baptist church. Moving to its present site in 1833, the church now occupies the oldest house of worship in the city. In the square stands a bronze likeness of General James Oglethorpe, founder of the Georgia colony, who was accompanied by at least one Baptist upon his initial voyage here.

FRANKLINTON, LOUISIANA
Half Moon Bluff Church Replica *(La. 10, 18; Washington Parish Fairgrounds—Mile Branch Settlement)*. It is the

first Baptist church organized in Louisiana, (Oct. 12, 1812) and the first non-Catholic church outside New Orleans in Louisiana. Although no organized congregation still exists, a replica of the building with its puncheon benches can be viewed on the fairgrounds along with original buildings of the period.

CLINTON, MISSISSIPPI
• **Mississippi College** (*West College Street*). Founded by Baptists in 1826, it is the oldest institution of higher education in the state. In 1831, it began granting degrees to women, one of earliest colleges to do so. The old chapel was used by Union troops as hospital and stable in their march on Vicksburg.
• **First Church** (*100 East College Street*). B.D. Gray, later HMB president, once pastored here, where his wife founded the first Sunbeams in the state of Mississippi.

SHILOH, NORTH CAROLINA
Shiloh Church (*N.C. Rte. 343, 12 miles south of U.S. 158*). On a peninsula between Elizabeth City and the Outer Banks is the oldest, but not quite the first, Baptist church in the state. Baptist settlers began arriving in the 1660s, some gathering for worship. But the first church was organized by Paul Palmer, who came in 1720; it didn't survive, but Palmer's second church, Shiloh, has. Palmer is considered "the father of General Baptists in North Carolina."

RICHMOND, VIRGINIA
First Church site (*East Broad and 12th streets*). Medical College of Virginia occupies the building which served First Baptist Church, 1839-1928. Here the SBC met in 1888 while the WMU was organized. Also, the Foreign Mission Board had offices here for a quarter-century, beginning in 1847, when the Board's first president, J. B. Jeter, also pastored the church. Several other executives of the Foreign Mission Board were leaders in this church, as well as several in home missions: Isaac Taylor Hinton, one of the first missionaries appointed by the Home Board, was ordained by and served as pastor of the church (1833-35) and J. Lewis Shuck, first missionary to the Chinese in California, was ordained here. Memorial tablets for him and his wife, Henrietta Hall Shuck, have been placed in the present building of First Church (*Monument Avenue and the Boulevard*).

The Southwest

Missions to an Emerging West

THE HISTORY OF THE SOUTHWEST is a story of nations changing hands: from Indian nations to Statehood; from Spain to Mexico; from independent republics to, finally, the United States. The Spanish first conquered parts of Texas and New Mexico in the 1500s. But by the late 1700s, Americans from the Southeastern Seaboard and inland states such as Tennessee were moving into the territory.

Meanwhile, American Indians, evicted from their eastern homelands by the U.S. government, became Oklahoma's first settlers. In 1830 the government moved some tribes voluntarily, others forcefully: The Trail of Tears saw vast numbers of Cherokees marched from Georgia and Tennessee.

Cherokees from Georgia brought their own Baptist missionary, Duncan O'Bryant, but the first Baptist church in Oklahoma Territory was organized in 1832 at Ebenezer Station by a group of Creek Indians from Georgia.

Most of the Indian tribes were hostile toward White people, and Christianity spread slowly. With the Cherokee tribe Christianity made its greatest progress. Jessee Bushyhead, one of its leaders, became a Baptist preacher. Evan Jones served the Cherokee Christians as a translator and publisher of the Bible, *Pilgrim's Progress*, sermons and hymns. In 1844, Jones and Bushyhead began publishing the *Cherokee Messenger*, a Baptist newspaper, the first paper of any kind in Oklahoma.

To THE SOUTH, JOSEPH BAYS, born in North Carolina, may have preached the first Baptist sermon in Texas. Bays and his son fought at San Jacinto in Texas' war for independence from Mexico. Afterward Sam Houston, president of the Texas Republic and a Baptist, appointed him commissioner to the Cherokee Indians.

Another Baptist, Zacharius Morrell, came to Texas in 1835. He visited Baptist pioneers near the present town of Marlin, little suspecting that within a few weeks many of them would be slain by Comanche Indians. Morrell went back to Tennessee for his family, and upon returning to Texas in 1837, established the first regular missionary Baptist church in Texas — at Washington.

James Huckins, the first missionary appointed to Texas, organized the First Baptist Church of Houston. He reported that immigrants were pouring in at the rate of 50,000 a year. The first black church in Texas was organized by I.S. Campbell, sent by the Ohio convention.

Over the years, five groups of Baptists evolved in Texas. But they united after a study committee, gathered by B.H. Carroll, pastor of First Baptist Church of Waco, ironed out differences.

Westward, Santa Fe had been established before the Pilgrims landed at Plymouth Rock. But the first Baptist sermon was not preached in New Mexico until two and a half centuries later, after the area had become a territory of the United States.

Hiram W. Read, a missionary appointed by the American Baptist Home Mission Society, established the first Baptist church in Albuquerque. Besides ministering to Army personnel, Read and others made evangelistic efforts among Hispanics and Indians. But during the Civil War their work declined.

By 1866 all Baptist missionaires had withdrawn from the territory. Churches ceased operations and

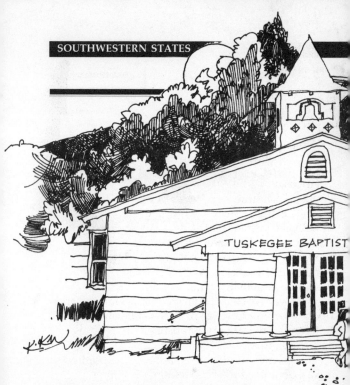

TUSKEGEE BAPTIST

were not reestablished until the 1880s.
By 1890 Baptist "affiliates" in New Mexico
numbered only 325.

In 1910, when a resolution failed to allow
churches the option to be affiliated with either
Northern or Southern Baptists, those with southern
interests withdrew and formed their own convention. The pain of separation prompted the establishment of a joint committee of both Baptist bodies
which, observing that New Mexico was being
populated by people principally from Texas and
other southern states, recommended that a new
convention be organized and affiliated with the
Southern Baptist Convention. In 1912, the two
groups re-merged, constituting the present state
convention.

In the few years between the Gasden Purchase
(1853) and the Civil War, settlers, mostly prospectors from southern states, moved into Arizona. In
the fall of 1875, James Bristow of Missouri, under a

cottonwood tree near Prescott, preached the first known Baptist sermon in the territory. The first Baptist church, Lone Star, was founded there.

More than 30 Baptist churches had been founded when Arizona was granted statehood in 1912. Arizona churches met in 1928 to constitute their own state convention, which eventually became parent/sponsor to churches in nine states to the north, all the way to the Canadian border. By the mid-fifties, nearly half of the 219 SBC churches in Arizona convention were outside the state, covering about one-fourth of the land area of the continental United States.

Subsequently, these churches developed four new conventions, from Colorado to Montana, and the work began so simply had spread to thousands of people, eloquent testimony to the steadfast faith of Baptists' pioneer forebears.

Independence, Texas

TEX

Independence Church and Museum

County Rd. 50, north of Brenham
Phone: 409/836-5117
Sunday Worship: 11 a.m.
Museum: 10 a.m.—4 p.m. Wednesday to Saturday,
*   1 p.m.—5 p.m. Sunday.*

ESTABLISHED IN 1839, this church is the oldest in continuous existence in Texas. In 1824, Independence was founded on land patented by Mexico to one of Texas' first families. The church was started 15 years later. Its first building burned and was replaced by the present structure in 1872. Six years later, the first Texas Home Mission Society was founded, with Baylor women as officers.

Many important names in Texas Baptist history were on the membership rolls of the church, but its most famous member was Gen. Sam Houston, leader of the forces that defeated Mexico and first president of the Republic of Texas.

Houston's wife, Margaret Lea, was a long-time member. In 1854, Houston was baptized by Dr. R.C. Burleson in the waters of Rocky Creek, south of the church.

The bell, which hung in the tower beside the church for 113 years, fell in 1969. The restored bell is in the nearby Texas Baptist Historical Museum.

The church's historic building is used as the Texas Baptist Historical Center.

A cemetery about a mile northwest of the church contains many historic graves and markers.

When Baylor University was chartered here in 1845, becoming the first university in the Southwest and the first Baptist school west of the Mississippi, its faculty and students worshipped in Independence church. After four decades, the school moved to Waco. The columns of the Female Department, standing among moss-hung oaks, are all that remain of Baylor's original buildings.

First Mexican Baptist Church
1232 South Alamo Street
Phone: 512/227-7982
Sunday Worship: 11 a.m. and 7 p.m.

WITHIN FIVE YEARS after Mexican Baptist work began in Laredo, W. D. Powell, a Mexico-based missionary, preached a revival here. Many Mexican-Americans were converted. Under his leadership, they organized in 1888 Primera Iglesia Bautista Mexicana; this is the oldest Spanish-speaking church in existence.

Here in 1910 was organized the Convencion Bautista Mexicana (Mexican Baptist Convention), which now functions as a part of the Texas Baptist Convention.

The Mexican Baptist Children's Home had its start in 1944, when three homeless children came to live in the parsonage of the church.

Central Baptist Church
1226 South Presa
Phone: 512/533-5882
Sunday Worship: 11 a.m.

HERE AT AGE 12, "PEEWEE" RUTLEDGE stepped out of the second row to become a Christian. He later was ordained in this church, which he pastored from 1942 to 1945.

An avid baseball player, Peewee played with Anglo and Mexican-American friends, establishing a pattern of racial openness that allowed the adult Arthur B. Rutledge, as president of the HMB during the turbulent 1960s and early '70s, to make the agency a beacon for racial justice and harmony.

El Paso, Texas

OKLAHOMA

TEXAS

Casa Bautista de Publicaciones
(Spanish-Baptist Publishing House)
7000 Alabama Street
Phone: 915/566-9656
Hours: 8 a.m.—5 p.m.

S PANISH BAPTIST PUBLISHING HOUSE operates
its various presses in facilites opened in 1919
by the Home Mission Board as a tuberculo-
sis sanitorium. With economic reverses, the
Sanitorium was forced to close 18 years later.

Meanwhile, the Spanish Publishing House,
founded in Mexico by the Foreign Mission Board,
retreated north of the border during a revolution in
the 1930s. In 1937, the Home Board exchanged
property with the Foreign Board, providing a permanent home for what would become the world's
largest publisher of evangelical literature in the
Spanish language.

The International WMU Publications Program
was transferred here in 1961.

Providing printed materials to more than 40
countries, Casa Bautista is just one of 38 publication
centers around the world operated by the Foreign
Mission Board.

Atoka, Oklahoma

First Baptist Church
123 North Delaware Street
Phone: 405/889-6633
Sunday Worship: 11 a.m. and 7 p.m.

AT BOGGY DEPOT, a few miles southwest of Atoka, this church was organized in 1869 by missionary to the Indians, Joseph Samuel Murrow, a Georgia native appointed in 1857 by the Southern Baptist Board of Domestic Missions (HMB).

It is the oldest Baptist church in Oklahoma with continuous service.

Here in 1872 was organized the Choctaw-Chickasaw Association, which was concluded with a communion service "to the mutual enjoyment and edification of every one. . . . There were White brethren, Red brethren and Black brethren, each feeling a deep interest in a common cause, and each rejoicing through the operation of the same Spirit."

Atoka Cemetery
Off U.S. 75 and Okla. Rte. 3

BURIED HERE IS MURROW (1835-1929), who helped found the Baptist association, the Indian Territory Convention, the Atoka Baptist Academy, Bacone College and "the only Christian orphanage in existence primarily for Indians."

Eufaula, Oklahoma

Tuskegee Baptist Church
*Mill Creek Road, approx. 1 mile south of Okla. Rte. 9
    and 6 miles west of town*
Sunday Worship: 11 a.m.

AFTER ANNIE ARMSTRONG organized the Woman's Baptist Home Mission Society of Maryland in 1882, her first project was to collect money and clothing for Indian students. Traveling by horseback and wagon, she first visited Indian Territory in 1900, travelling 4,000 miles in 40 days to visit mission points and organize women's societies.

On the grounds of the church, organized in 1856 and still meeting today, is a rock from which Miss Armstrong is said to have mounted her horse for the long journey.

In the next five years, she visited the area four more times — her 1902 trip taking 80 days and covering 8,500 miles. After hearing Miss Annie speak, a frontier woman remarked: "I no longer belong only to this little town, but I feel I am a part of God's great universe."

Greenwood Cemetery
Near U.S. 69, north edge of Eufaula

IN THE BUCKNER FAMILY PLOT is buried Henry Frieland Buckner (1818-1882), who came with his family in 1849 as a missionary to the "hostile" Creek Nation. Indeed, one of Mrs. Buckner's first tasks was to clean the blood of a murdered man from the floor of their new home.

By 1853, Buckner had established a mission at Eufaula, and, except for the Civil War years, he remained here until his death. During that time, he produced a Creek-language grammar, hymnal and New Testament, which were published by the Board of Domestic and Indian Missions (HMB) under whose appointment he served.

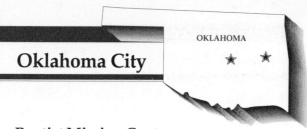
Baptist Mission Center
2125 Exchange Street
Phone: 405/235-6162
Hours: Please call before visiting.

IN THIS HISPANIC NEIGHBORHOOD, the WMU of First Baptist Church began in 1917 a day-care service for workers of the meat-packing plant. As the women became aware of needs in the community, they expanded their mission action and constructed their first building here in 1926. A second building was added four decades later. Both buildings continue to house the center.

In 1971, management of the center was assumed by the Association, with cooperative support from the state convention and the Home Mission Board.

The work of the center, while still serving the immediate community, includes all of Oklahoma City. The center annually distributes more than 40,000 pieces of clothing and provides food to more than 6,000. Hundreds receive free medical and dental care.

Each year, Vacation Bible schools and other ministries are offered with the help of 15 to 20 student summer missionaries.

Fruitland, New Mexico

Fruitland Mission
Old U.S. 550
Phone: 505/598-5593
Sunday Worship: 11 a.m. and 7 p.m.

A MAJOR CENTER OF BAPTIST WORK among Navajo Indians is at the edge of their reservation, the largest in the U.S. with some 16 million acres and more than 75,000 residents. In 1976, Kenneth and Rose Norton, a Navajo couple appointed by the Home Mission Board, came to the 18-year-old mission at Fruitland.

The only person to attend their first Sunday service was an old grandmother; she brought her granddaughter the next service, but the Nortons realized the mission was on verge of collapse, which the first Southern Baptist Navajo mission did (Farmington, 1941).

The Nortons have worked hard, however, to revitalize and expand the Baptist witness. As their congregation grew, a new sanctuary was constructed in 1986. The Nortons began a radio ministry and another mission southwest of Shiprock.

As resources permit, the Fruitland Mission also distributes food and clothing to the needy; its facilities have showers which Indians may use as they travel to and from the reservation.

Las Vegas, N.M.

NEW MEXICO

First Baptist Church
Seventh and University
Phone: 505/425-7125
Sunday Worship: 11 a.m. and
6 p.m. (winter), 7 p.m. (summer)

THIS IS THE OLDEST BAPTIST CHURCH in the state. Following the Civil War, Southern Baptist missionaries withdrew from the territory. When they returned more than a decade later, they had to establish new work altogether. The first was the church at Las Vegas, founded with 20 charter members on Jan. 1, 1880.

When Mina Everett was appointed as a missionary to New Mexico in 1901, she helped organize the first Spanish-speaking Baptist congregation as a mission of this church. Ms. Everett, "one of the Kingdom's choicest women," was originally sent to New Mexico by the Woman's Baptist Home Mission Society in Chicago. With experience in organizing Baptist women's work in Texas, she led in forming the first New Mexico Woman's Missionary Union, and served as its corresponding secretary.

An early pastor of First Church was Blas Chavez (1829-1907), the first Hispanic Baptist convert in the state, who was baptized by Samuel Gorman. Chavez became the "El Gran Viejo" (Grand Old Man) of New Mexico Baptist life during his ministry, which spanned six decades.

Sacaton, Arizona

First Pima Church
Santan Road, off Ariz. Rte. 87, 10 miles west of town
Phone: 602/562-3449
Sunday Worship: 11 a.m. and 6 p.m.

ARIZONA'S FIRST INDIAN BAPTIST church resulted from a Baptist couple teaching in a Presbyterian Bible class. Missourians J. O. Willett and his wife had moved to Arizona in 1918 for health reasons, where they operated Four Mile Trading Post near the Pima Indian Reservation. Because no Baptist work was yet established, the Willietts attended the Presbyterian church.

An ordained minister, Willett was asked to teach Indians in Sunday School. However, when the Willetts did not sway from teaching their Baptist views on regeneration and baptism, the church asked them to quit the class.

Intent on becoming Baptists, the Indians also left. Together they organized in 1922 as a Baptist mission, which for a few months was sponsored by the First Southern Church in Phoenix. On Thanksgiving Eve, 1925, the Sacaton congregation constituted into a church.

Willett (1867-1954) later served as first president of the Arizona Southern Baptist convention.

C. Frank Frazier (1888-1964) later became pastor of the church. Appointed by the Home Mission Board, he was the first Southern Baptist missionary among the Pimas and Papagos.

Behind the adobe church, Frazier and his wife are buried in the old Indian cemetery — quite an honor for Whites. His wife's grave is unmarked just outside the wooden fence encompassing his grave.

Tucson, Arizona

ARIZONA

Friendship Center
848 South 9th Street
Phone: 602/ 624- 6000
Please phone for an appointment before visiting.

THE FIRST CHRISTIAN community ministries program in the state was initiated in 1970 by Ross and Betty Jane Hanna, who for 14 years had been home missionaries to Indians in Oklahoma, New Mexico and Arizona. Their work now includes two other centers, Pascua Activities Center *(850 West Calle Sur)* and Manzo Activities Center *(1346 West Sonora)*, all operating under the name Sharing Ministries.

Pascua Village, on Tucson's outskirts, was settled by the Yaqui Indians. In 1972, Hanna with the chairman of the tribe, rode along the unpaved streets, with no lamps or sewer system. The chairman said that he wanted Hanna to start a center in Pascua like the Friendship Center, but that the Hannas would have to work a year with the people before talking about religion. Hanna agreed.

Within that year he won the confidence of the people. Today the center communicates the love of Christ both verbally and physically.

In addition to worship services, the centers offer a wide range of ministries, including medical help, food and clothing distribution, children's learning programs, literacy and adult education.

Other Sites of Interest

PHOENIX, ARIZONA

• **First Chinese Church** *(4910 East Earll Drive)*. Among the earliest non-Hispanic language mission work in the Southwest was a Chinese mission started by Central Baptist Church in 1938. The present building, purchased in 1944, was a Jewish synagogue to which a baptistry and other renovations were added after home missionary Lawrence Stanley became pastor. Dr. Stanley, having pastored the Chinese Church in San Antonio, Texas, for 10 years, served the Chinese here in the "Valley of the Sun" for 30 more years.

• **First Southern Church** *(3100 West Camelback Road)*. Organized in March, 1921, this was the first Southern Baptist church in the state. In September, 1925, First and six other Arizona SBC churches formed their own association, from which evolved the state Southern Baptist convention. With Home Mission Board support, the Arizona convention served as sponsor of many SBC missions started in the west during the 1950s and early 1960s. The state now has more than 250 SBC churches.

ESPANOLA, NEW MEXICO

Santa Clara Indian Mission *(N.M. Rte. 30, about 3 miles south of town)*. On the west bank of the Rio Grande is Santa Clara Pueblo, the first to include a Baptist building. Today's work is attributed to home missionary Pauline Cammack, who established a kindergarten in the home of an Indian, Rose Naranjo. Rose became a Christian, then her husband Mike. Eventually they served as Indian missionaries, with Mike helping establish the mission congregation, building the clay meeting house and serving as first pastor, 1950-55.

WESTVILLE, OKLAHOMA

Baptist Town Mission site *(U.S. 59, about 4 miles north of town)*. Approximately 1,000 Cherokees led by Jesse Bushyhead settled near here in 1839 "at a place called Baptist." Within a couple of years arrived Evan Jones, a missionary who had worked with the Cherokees in Georgia. The first newspaper of any kind published in Oklahoma, *The Cherokee Messenger*, was started by Bushyhead and Jones. Because of his outspoken criticism of the Indian Removal program, Jones was forbidden to preach by the federal government.

Bushyhead preached in his place and until his death in 1844, worked closely with Jones. Bushyhead is buried in the church cemetery across the highway from the Old Baptist Mission Church, the first Indian Baptist church in the state (now affiliated with a Landmark association).

DALLAS, TEXAS
Buckner Baptist Children's Home *(5200 South Buckner Blvd., approx. 1/2 mile south of I-30)*. On the campus of the Buckner Home are the offices of Buckner Baptist Benevolences, a multi-service Christian social care organization founded in 1879. A network of childcare and family services, Buckner helps 2,100 children a year on five campuses and in 10 satellite operations. On the grounds is the log cabin of founder R. C. Buckner, nephew of the famed Indian missionary H. F. Buckner.

GALVESTON, TEXAS
First Baptist Church *(Sealy Street between 22nd and 23rd Streets)*. This 1958 building is the fourth occupied by the first Baptist congregation in the city, organized Jan. 30, 1840, in the home of Tom Borden. Along with their wives, Tom and his brother Gail, famous inventor of the method for condensed milk, were charter members under the leadership of James Huckins, one of the first six missionaries of the Home Mission Board. In early days, Huckins wrote: "The Methodist and Presbyterian ministers treat me with all affection of brothers. They are Christian gentlemen. . . . We have a ministers' meeting every Monday morning, for prayer — for ascertaining the progress of the gospel in the city — and for devising modes of attack upon the bulwarks of Satan. We take our stand side by side."

North Central States

Baptist Post-War Growth

BAPTISTS MOVED WEST as the new nation stretched beyond the original 13 Colonies. Much of the movement's wellspring was Kentucky. Many settlers to Indiana immigrated from Kentucky, in the 1790s, bringing with them their Baptist faith. They established the first Baptist church in Indiana — Silver Creek Baptist Church. Other churches were begun and Baptist work spread. The Great Awakening fueled growth of Indiana churches under the leadership of such men as Isaac McCoy, who worked primarily with Indians, and Squire Boone, a Baptist preacher and brother to Daniel.

James Smith, a Baptist preacher from Kentucky, started the first mission in Illinois in 1787, preaching the first non-Catholic sermon in the "wilderness." Soon Baptist churches were springing up throughout Illinois, the earliest being New Design Baptist Church in 1796.

Baptists from Illinois soon moved into Iowa, founding the first Baptist church at Danville in 1834.

MEANWHILE, BAPTISTS WERE AMONG the first non-Catholic Whites to settle west of the Mississippi. In 1796 Baptist Thomas Bull and his family settled in Cape Girardeau County, outside St. Louis. Others joined them the following year for study of Scriptures, singing and prayers.

After 1803, with the Louisiana Purchase and the religious liberty which the Baptists of New England and Virginia had fought for and gained in the new U.S. Constitution, Baptists were free to start churches in Missouri. The first was Tywappity Church, organized in 1805.

John Mason Peck and James Welches arrived as missionaries to the Missouri Territory in 1819. They preached, taught school, organized churches and female "mite" societies in Missouri and neighbor-

ing Illinois. The first missionary society in the west, The United Society for the Spread of the Gospel, was organized in 1818. Peck later supported himself bi-vocationally and in 1822 was given five dollars a week for support by the Massachusetts Baptist Missionary Society.

WHILE A FEW CHURCHES ASSOCIATED with the Southern Baptist Convention before modern times (such as Indiana's Memorial Baptist Church, begun in 1861 by German-speaking immigrants, which affiliated in the early part of the century), Southern Baptists were late comers to the midwest, and their origins were of a grassroots movement growing out of post-World War II migration patterns, as thousands of southerners sought jobs in the industrial states.

With the exception of the Missouri Baptist Convention (the Baptist Central Society of Missouri was started in 1835), state conventions were not established until the twentieth century: Illinois, with its heavy concentration of SBC churches in the southern part of the state, came in 1910. But the rest resulted from the Convention's "Pioneer Movement" into the North Central States: Ohio, 1954; Michigan, 1957, Indiana, 1958; and Minnesota-Wisconsin, 1984.

Vincennes, Indiana

Maria Creek Baptist Church
On campus of Vincennes State University
To visit inside the building,
  please call: 812/885-4364

I N 1809 REV. ISAAC McCOY gathered his first
congregation of Baptists, who had begun
moving into the state from Kentucky in the
1790s. McCoy, who was to become the leader
of Baptist Indian Missions in the "West" (today's
Midwest) was ordained here and served as pastor
from 1809 to 1818.

In 1809, an association was formed near Vincennes.

The Great Awakening fueled growth of churches
in Indiana, under the leadership of such men as
McCoy, who worked primarily with the Indians,
Judge Jesse Holman, and Squire Boone, brother to
Daniel and a Baptist preacher, until controversy
and anti-mission sentiment in the 1820s stopped the
movement.

The mission-minded McCoy moved on. Near
Chicago, as a missionary of the Triennial Convention, McCoy preached the first sermon in English,
about 1822. In 1826, McCoy resigned as a missionary of the Triennial Convention to concentrate on
Indian work. He had already established, in 1822,
the first Baptist Indian Mission in Michigan among
the Potawatomies, a few miles west of Niles. He
went on to begin Indian missions from Northern
Arkansas to Kansas.

The restored Maria Creek Church meeting house
is now a state landmark, housing a small museum
of McCoy memorabilia.

New Design, Illinois

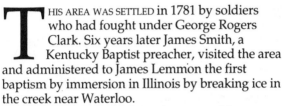

INDIANA

ILLINOIS

New Design Church site and Cemetery
Off State Hgwy. 3, 4 miles south of Waterloo

THIS AREA WAS SETTLED in 1781 by soldiers who had fought under George Rogers Clark. Six years later James Smith, a Kentucky Baptist preacher, visited the area and administered to James Lemmon the first baptism by immersion in Illinois by breaking ice in the creek near Waterloo.

A subsequent revival was interrupted by an Indian raid, but the community prospered with the first Baptist church being formed in 1796.

Lemmon, who is buried in the adjacent cemetery, became known as the first Baptist missionary in Illinois.

The first governor of Illinois, Shadrach Bond, was a member of the New Design Baptist Church when he was elected. He and James Lemmon were among those who wrote the Constitution for the state.

Mrs. Lillie Lemmon Leavitt, a granddaughter of Rev. Lemmon, was instrumental in organizing the state WMU in 1908. She was elected its first president, and she was a part of state and national mission work before the Illinois Baptist State Association was organized, being one of the convention speakers.

The original church building no longer stands, but there is an Illinois Baptist historical marker at the cemetery on the old church grounds.

Madison, Wisconsin

First Baptist Church
518 North Franklin Avenue
Phone: 608/233-1880
Sunday Worship: 11 a.m.

T HE CHURCH WAS FOUNDED in 1853, making it one of the early churches in the state. A prominent figure in the church's history was William H. Brisbane, a former South Carolina slaveholder, who was forced to leave the South when he manumitted his slaves. He came to pastor this congregation.

Midvale Baptist Church
821 South Midvale Boulevard
Phone: 608/233-5661
Sunday Worship: 11 a.m.

I N 1953, FOUR FAMILIES IN MADISON contacted an Illinois area missionary, Harold E. Cameron, requesting assistance to start a Southern Baptist church. Cameron was one of Southern Baptists' early church starters in the Midwest, helping start dozens of churches in the Illinois-Wisconsin area during the 1950s and 1960s, when Southern Baptists were expanding beyond their traditional southern-state boundaries.

Within weeks of the request, the Immanuel Church was founded, now Midvale, the first Southern Baptist congregation organized in the state.

Winterset, Iowa

First Baptist Church

210 East Jefferson
Phone: 515/462-1050
Sunday Worship: 11 a.m.

F IRST BUILT IN 1862, this is the oldest congregation in the Iowa Southern Baptist Fellowship. Originally affiliated with the
American Baptist Convention, it became an
independent church in 1955. After a study of
doctrine and practice, the church voted in 1962 to
align itself with the Southern Baptist Convention.
Here in 1965 was organized the statewide Iowa
Southern Baptist Association, which later became
the state fellowship.

The present building dates from 1905, when
materials where brought from the St. Louis World's
Fair to help rebuild the sanctuary after it was
destroyed by fire.

St. Joseph, Missouri

First Baptist Church
Thirteenth and Francis Streets
Phone: 816/232-8425
Sunday Worship: 11 a.m. and 7 p.m.

FOUNDED IN 1845, when the town was twice as large as Kansas City and a major departure point for the West, the church was instrumental in starting new works throughout northwestern Missouri.

But perhaps its most significant contribution was in 1933, when the pastor, Frank Tripp (1894-1975), suggested the idea of the Hundred Thousand Club to help Southern Baptist agencies alleviate their debt brought on by the Depression and other hardships. Approved by the SBC Executive Committee, the plan was for club members to give one extra dollar per month above their regular offerings. First Church continued Tripp's salary but allowed him to work full-time as the chief promotion officer to launch the campaign, which by the end of 1943 successfully eliminated the debts of the Southern Baptist Convention — and which has remained debt-free ever since.

The Executive Committee expressed gratitude to Tripp and First Church for their contributions to the club "which to a large extent saved our mission causes."

MISSOURI

Third Baptist Church
620 North Grand Boulevard
Phone: 314/533-7340
Sunday Worship: 10:40 a.m. and 7 p.m.

As J. B. JETER WAS LEAVING his pastorate at Second Church to return to his native Virginia, his ideas for planting more churches were finally coming to fruition. His congregation helped sponsor a new mission, organized in 1850 by Joseph Walker, a Pennsylvania native who three years later became the Corresponding secretary of the Home Mission Board.

The new church became one of the strongest in the state. Although dually aligned with American and Southern Baptists today, the church hosted the 1919 meeting which abolished the "Missouri Plan" of dual affiliation for the state Baptist association.

"With the clear and definite understanding that any individual or church preferring to co-operate with the Northern Baptist Convention is free to do so without hindrance or censure," the state body voted for single alignment with the Southern Baptist Convention. As a result, the Home Mission Board immediately assisted the state convention, increasing its evangelistic outreach significantly.

Other Sites of Interest

FORT WAYNE, INDIANA

Old Fort Wayne *(Rte. 33, North Clinton Street)*. Within the restored fort (a state historical site), visitors may see the original structure of First Baptist Church, founded by Isaac McCoy. *(For more on McCoy, see Vincennes, Indiana.)*

DANVILLE, IOWA

First Baptist Church *(302 South Main Street)*. Among the earliest pioneers in Iowa were William and Hephzibah Manly, a Kentucky couple who with a few settlers from Illinois organized the first Baptist church in the upper district of the Louisiana Purchase. On the evening of Oct. 19, 1834, they gathered in the log house of Noble Hously. Elder John Logan of Illinois preached to them the first evangelical sermon in the territory, and on the following day they constituted "the Regular Baptist Church at Long Creek." A centennial stone can be found at the present location of the church, now known as Danville First Church.

JACKSON, MICHIGAN

Gorham Church *(2692 North Dettman Road)*. Organized in 1910, as Memorial Baptist Mission and constituted as Gorham Street Church in 1923, four years later it affiliated with the Franklin Association of Illinois, becoming the first Southern Baptist church in the state.

BOLIVAR, MISSOURI

Southwest Baptist University *(1601 South Springfield Street)*. Established as a college in 1878, the university received aid under the Mountain Mission Schools program of the Home Mission Board from 1918 to 1929.

BRIDGETON, MISSOURI

Fee Fee Church *(11330 St. Charles Rock Road)*. Founded in 1807, this is the oldest church in continuous existence in the state, the oldest Baptist and oldest non-Catholic church west of the Mississippi River. Its organizer, Thomas R. Musick (1756-1842), is buried in Fee Fee Cemetery at the original site of the church *(2 miles southwest)*.

GRANDVIEW, MISSOURI
First Baptist Church *(15th and Main Streets)*. Harry S. Truman (1888-1972), 33rd President of the U.S., was a life-long member of the church founded by his southern forebears. On his 79th birthday, Truman was honored by the Southern Baptist Convention. He reportedly said that he had been to Baptist and Democratic Party Conventions, "and to tell you the truth, there's not much difference." Truman is buried at the Truman Library and Museum *(U.S. 24 and Delaware)* in Independence.

JACKSON, MISSOURI
Old Bethel Church site *(Mo. Rtes. 72 & 25, approx. 1.5 miles south of town)*. Organized by Rev. David Green in 1806, this was the second Baptist church in Missouri. Its meeting house, constructed of poplar logs, was the first Protestant church building west of the "Great River." From this church came other churches which together organized the Bethel Association in 1816, the first Baptist association west of the Mississippi. When anti-missionary sentiments gained a majority of the members, about 1826, a minority who were missionary-minded withdrew and organized their own church, First Church of Jackson *(212 South High Street)*.

HAMILTON, OHIO
Westside Baptist Church *(154 Gordon Avenue)*. Established in 1929, this was the first Southern Baptist church in Ohio. About 25 years later, in January 1954, messengers from 40 churches across the state met at Westside to constitute the State Convention of Baptists in Ohio.

MINNEAPOLIS, MINNESOTA
Southtown Baptist Church *(2600 W. 82nd Street)*. Three transplanted Southern Baptist families—from New Mexico, Missouri and Montana—received encouragement and advice from the Home Mission Board and Illinois Baptists to establish a church in the Twin Cities area. Founded in 1956 in the suburb of Bloomington, it is the first Southern Baptist church in the state.

The Great Plains

A New Era in Outreach

"I once thought to write a history of the immigrants in America," wrote one scholar. "Then I discovered that the immigrants were American history."

IN 1541 FRANCISCO CORONADO, in search of gold, marched with a small band of soldiers into present-day Nebraska. He found Indians who ate raw buffalo meat and lived in grass houses. He raised a cross and left. It was the first Christian cross raised in Nebraska.

Exploration further north came nearly 200 years later. In 1738 Pierre de la Verendrye made the land of the Sioux Indians part of France, who sold it to the United States in 1803. The area officially became the Dakota territory in 1861. Despite the early establishment of army outposts and the arrival of Missouri River steamboats (1832), the region did not attract many settlers until eastern farmers heard reports of 40 bushels of wheat per acre. They were followed by immigrant farmers from Scandinavia, Russia and Germany. In 1873, the railroad brought others, especially after gold was discovered in 1874. The non-Indian population rose from 15,000 in 1870 to 135,000 only ten years later.

The first known Baptists in Dakota Territory, Elijah Terry and James Tanner, arrived in 1852 at Walhalla, North Dakota. Baptist churches were started at Yankton, South Dakota, in 1864 and in Fargo, North Dakota, in 1879. Baptist missionaries in the territory numbered only half dozen before the advent of the railroad in 1873. But by 1881, the American Baptist Home Mission Society had appointed 48.

These missionaries helped establish various language churches. As the ethnic populations (Swedes, Norwegians, Germans and Danes) became Americanized, they adopted English for their worship services.

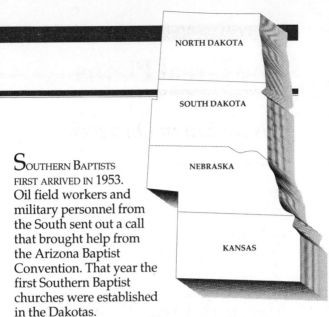

NORTH DAKOTA

SOUTH DAKOTA

NEBRASKA

KANSAS

Southern Baptists first arrived in 1953. Oil field workers and military personnel from the South sent out a call that brought help from the Arizona Baptist Convention. That year the first Southern Baptist churches were established in the Dakotas.

The work rapidly expanded. In 1958 the Home Mission Board appointed missionaries to North Dakota. Congregations were organized and met in homes, civic buildings, hotels and other places. Some pastors worked as many as six preaching stations and traveled a thousand miles a week. By 1967 this energetic start had resulted in enough churches in the Dakotas, Wyoming and Montana that together they organized the Northern Plains Baptist Convention.

In 1984, Wyoming churches formed their own separate convention. And with continued growth the Northern Plains convention dissolved in 1988, as Montana and Dakota churches established separate fellowships, each in anticipation of their own convention.

Baptist work further south, in Kansas and Nebraska, traces its roots to missions to American Indians.

In Kansas, Isaac McCoy, the legendary missionary, founded the American Indian Mission Association in 1842. Later it came under direction of the Board of Domestic Missions of the Southern Baptist Convention.

McCoy consistently worked to see that Indians

A New Era in Outreach

were fairly treated by the government. In Kansas he defined areas for relocation of Indian tribes, laid out plans for cities and initiated Baptist missions at Topeka and at Paaoli.

The Indian work phased out as Indian people began attending English-speaking churches, and from the Civil War until the turn of the century, Baptist missions were supported largely by American Baptists.

In the early 1900s some Kansas churches along the borders of Missouri and Oklahoma began to affiliate with those SBC state conventions. The Kansas Convention of Southern Baptists was organized in 1947.

The first Baptist work in Nebraska was started

Baptist Mission

in 1833. Moses Merrill and his wife drove an ox team to a village on the Missouri River and started a mission with the Otoe and Missouri Indians. Merrill published a book of hymns in the Otoe language.

The first Southern Baptist church in Nebraska came more than a century later, being organized in Lincoln in 1955. The following year the First Baptist Church of Kimball was started. Churches then developed rapidly. As more and more Nebraska churches affiliated with the Kansas convention, the name was changed to the Kansas-Nebraska Convention.

An important site of pioneer missionary Isaac McCoy's Indian mission work is found in Topeka, Kansas.

the Pottawatomie

Kansas City, Kansas

SOUTH DAKOTA

NEBRASKA

KANSAS

Shawnee Mission site
51st and Walmer Streets, south of I-35

REV. ISAAC MCCOY, exploring in 1829, obtained permission from the Shawnee chief to continue mission work among his people after they moved here as the first immigrant Indians in Kansas. McCoy chose a site south of the Methodist mission, and in 1831, Dr. Johnston Lykins and his wife, Delilah, daughter of McCoy, arrived to begin the work. They began operating as a church by August, 1832, the first Baptist church in Kansas.

The first printing press in Kansas was at the mission. Operated by Jotham Meeker, it was used to publish the *Siwinowe Kesibwi* (*Shawnee Sun*), a newspaper in the Shawnee language which Lykins helped to edit. The press produced items in other Indian languages for several mission stations.

The Shawnee Baptist Mission served as a training field, or first stop, for many early Baptist missionaries to the Indians of the West.

An historical marker has been placed in the vicinity of this important mission.

Central Baptist Theological Seminary
Seminary Heights
31st and Minnesota Avenues
Phone: 913/371-5313

FOUNDED IN 1901, THE SEMINARY was jointly sponsored by Southern and Northern (American) Baptist Conventions until Southern Baptists opened their own school across the river in Missouri in 1957. The library at Central contains materials related to Indian missions, including a collection related to Charles Journeycake, a Baptist minister who was the last chief of the Delawares.

Calvary Baptist Church
4601 Mount Rushmore Road
Phone: 605/342-3384
Sunday Worship: 10:45 a.m.-7

THE FIRST SOUTHERN BAPTIST congregation in the state was begun by military personnel from Ellsworth Air Force Base who wanted a church with strong missionary and evangelistic programs. Under the leadership of L.A. Watson, general missionary for the Arizona convention, they constituted into a church on March 25, 1953.

Within a few months, they were called upon to support a group at Sturgis Air Force Base, and most of the churches subsequently established throughout the state were related, or touched at least indirectly, through the outreach of Calvary Church.

In November, 1967, a meeting here was called by the Colorado Baptist General Convention and the Home Mission Board for the purpose of organizing the Northern Plains Baptist Convention.

Other Sites of Interest

BELLVUE, NEBRASKA

Oto Mission (*historical marker on Rte. 75, 10 miles west of Omaha*). Near a farm house three miles west of the marker is a stone chimney, only physical remains of the mission for Oto Indians begun by Moses Merrill in 1833. Merrill experienced opposition from whiskey-selling trading post operators, but the Indians called him "The-One-Who-Always-Speaks-Truth." He died in 1839 and is buried on the banks of the Missouri River.

LINCOLN, NEBRASKA

Southview Church (*3434 South 13th Street*). Air Force personnel in this area after World War II saw many crosses but none over a Southern Baptist church. Meeting Easter Sunday, 1955, in a sergeant's home, a group began what developed into the first Southern Baptist church in the state.

OMAHA, NEBRASKA

Omaha Baptist Center (*504 N. 22nd Street*). Home missionary Alene Lockwood won the hearts of children in a 1963 Bible school. At their pleas, she stayed and with the help of local churches began a weekday and Sunday program. By the following year, with the support of the Home Mission Board, property was purchased and the ministry expanded. It now ministers to Anglo, Black, Hispanic and American Indian residents with the motto: "There is not a task before us as great as the power behind us."

BURDEN, KANSAS

First Southern Baptist Church (*Kan. Rte. 15*). Messengers from across the state met at First Church in 1945, to organize the Kansas Southern Baptist Fellowship, forerunner of the Kansas-Nebraska Fellowship. The next year, the church also served as the site for the first annual meeting of the Kansas WMU.

LANSING, KANSAS

First Baptist Church (*U.S. 73, 2 miles south of Kan. Rte. 5*). One of the first White churches in Kansas, and now affiliated with American Baptists, the church was organized by two Southern Baptist ministers in 1856.

Originally located two miles east, the congregation was first known as the Delaware City Church, and the salary of its pastor, Rev. W. Thomas, was supplied by the Home Mission Board. In October, 1858, Thomas helped organize the East Kansas Baptist Association, but shortly thereafter he moved to Austin, Texas. The other founding minister, South Carolinian Winfield Scott, became pastor in 1866. The name of the church was changed to Nine Mile Creek, then to Bethel. Eventually its present site and name were adopted.

TOPEKA, KANSAS
Pottawatomie Baptist Mission Site *(Kansas State Museum and Archives, Irish Road, 6425 SW 6, 1/2 mile off I-70)*. The stone barn is the actual mission site of pioneer Indian missionary Isaac McCoy's work with the Pottawatomie tribe. His papers are in the collection. *(For more on McCoy, see Vincennes, Indiana.)*

BISMARCK, NORTH DAKOTA
Capitol Heights Church *(U.S. 83 & Divide Avenue)*. Just northeast of the Capitol is the second oldest Southern Baptist church in the state, begun in the fall of 1954 by area missionary O.R. "Benny" Delmar. Prior to Capitol Heights' constitution in December, an organ was loaned to the mission by a Roman Catholic priest who observed, "You Baptists are meeting the heart's hunger that no other group is meeting. . . . Bismarck needs your ministry as well as the whole state of North Dakota." *(For more on Delmar, see Casper, Wyoming.)*

DICKINSON, NORTH DAKOTA
First Baptist Church *(N.D. Rte. 22 and U.S. 10)*. The oldest Southern Baptist church now existing in North Dakota was begun in June, 1954. Initially meeting in the basement of the community building, the Dickinson congregation called as its first pastor, J. H. Brister of Roswell, N.M. Under his leadership the church grew strong enough to purchase and renovate an Episcopal church building, to which they added a baptistry.

Rocky Mountains

Churches for a Rugged Land

OTHER THAN MORMONS AND FUR TRADERS, few U.S. citizens had interest in the mountain states—until the discovery of silver and gold. And Baptists were right there with the miners, prospectors and ranchers to tame the wild west. Interest in Montana was awakened with the discovery of gold, 1852-1864, and communities sprung up such as Grasshopper Creek and Last Chance Gulch. In Virginia City, the territorial capital, an expedition party with a Baptist cook arrived in about 1865. The cook founded the first Baptist church in Montana Territory.

Southern Baptists were among those who migrated here during the industrial developments following World War II. An oil field worker who had transferred from Oklahoma helped establish the first Southern Baptist church at Billings. In rapid succession many other churches were established throughout the state, and missions began on the Indian reservations.

BETWEEN 1840 AND THE OUTBREAK of the Civil War, some 150,000 westward-bound travelers crossed through Wyoming, between the outposts of Fort Laramie and Fort Bridger.

In 1870, little more than a year after Congress created the Wyoming Territory, the first Baptist missionary arrived in Laramie.

The discovery of oil in the 1920s caused the state's first real growth spurt, as oil field workers, many from Texas and Oklahoma, moved in. One Southern Baptist family persuaded their former pastor, O.R. "Benny" Delmar, to visit. Delmar led a revival at Casper that resulted in the first Southern Baptist church in Wyoming.

A year later three missions were started in the state. These and other new Wyoming churches affiliated with the Colorado convention when it organized in 1956. The Wyoming Southern Baptist Convention was formed in 1984.

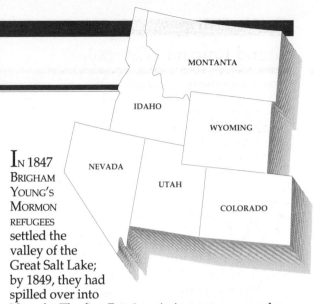

In 1847 Brigham Young's Mormon refugees settled the valley of the Great Salt Lake; by 1849, they had spilled over into Nevada. The first Baptist missionary was preaching to a congregation in the terrritory in 1864, but local resistance kept Baptist work small. Utah's first Southern Baptist church was not founded until 1944 — in Roosevelt.

Nevada Baptists were hindered by disruptions of war, frontier bandits and difficulty of travel between towns. But their dedication gradually planted an evangelical witness.

Southern Baptists entered Nevada amid a World War II-created mining boom. In 1947, two deacons among military personnel at Babbit founded a church, which invited help of the Home Mission Board. In 1978 the Nevada Baptist Convention was formed with 71 churches.

Gold was discovered in the Denver area in 1858. The new boomtown mining camps had little law and order—a common saying was, "There is no Sunday west of Junction City and no God west of Salina (Kansas)."

Baptists, however, were not long coming. Baptist minister William Whitehead founded the first Baptist church in the territory at Golden.

A few Southern Baptist churches were started in the 1930s. In 1955 messengers from 90 churches across five states organized the Colorado Baptist General Convention, which lasted until 1968, when Northern Plains Baptists formed their own convention, leaving Colorado a one-state convention.

Grand Junction, Colorado

Bookcliff Church
2702 Patterson Road
Phone: 303/243-9285
Sunday Worship: 11 a.m. and 7 p.m.

WHEN HARRY STAGG, executive director of the New Mexico Convention, received urgent calls from Grand Junction, he sent associational missionary Solon Brown with other pastors to hold four simultaneous revivals. They met with community opposition, but the pastors declared that they were there "not by comity, nor council of churches, but because of the Great Commission."

From their results developed the first Southern Baptist church in the town. A month before it was constituted in November, 1950, secretaries from the New Mexico WMU, Eva Inlow and Bernice Elliott, came and organized the first Southern Baptist WMU in the state.

Riverside Center
505 North 18th
Phone: 303/243-8541

EDDIE AND JUNE SCROGGINS first came to Grand Junction in 1955, when he was called to pastor Trinity Church. Some years later, he and his wife returned here to begin a Baptist center, offering literacy education, family crisis counseling, clothing distribution, music activities, Girls in Action and Mission Friends. From the worship opportunities provided has grown a congregation organized in 1982 as the Riverside Church.

Casper, Wyoming

WYOMING

COLORADO

First Southern
Baptist Church
220 South Pennsylvania
Phone: 307/265-6540
Sunday Worship: 11 a.m.
and 7 p.m.

T HE FIRST SOUTHERN BAPTIST CHURCH in the
state came about when O. R. "Benny"
Delmar, on his way to the 1951 Southern
Baptist Convention in San Francisco,
preached a revival here at the request of some oil-
field workers and their families. As a result, the
congregation met in the city-county building and
constituted themselves as a church the following
month, calling Delmar as their pastor.

Delmar came and also served as an area missionary, becoming one of the greatest church-
starting missionaries in Southern Baptist history.
First Southern, over the next quarter century, was
mother, grandmother or great-grandmother to
more than 100 SBC congregations; Delmar was
responsible for many of their beginnings.

At this same church in October, 1983, the Wyoming Fellowship of Southern Baptist Churches met
and recommended constitution of their own state
convention. The next month, the Northern Plains
Convention held its 16th annual session here and
granted formal approval to the new body.

The WMU, organized with the Wyoming Southern Baptist Convention, named its state missions
week of prayer in honor of Delmar.

Brockton, Montana

Brockton Baptist Mission
In the middle of town, Rte. 404 and U.S. 2
Sunday Worship: 11 a.m.

S OUTHERN BAPTIST WORK among the Assiniboin
and Dakota (Sioux) Indians began in 1956
when Rev. A. L. Davis and his wife,
Gladys, were living on Fort Peck Reservation. With the help of two Arkansas young women
sent by the Home Mission Board under the Tent-
maker program, they conducted at Wolf Point a
Vacation Bible School, the first ever held on the
reservation.

While pastoring First Baptist Church of Poplar
in 1957, Davis established a mission at Brockton in
the home of Britain Fast Horse, where he held
Sunday afternoon and Tuesday evening services.

Eventually a lot was purchased for the Indian
mission and a Lutheran chapel building in Poplar
was purchased for $100.00 and moved to this site.

The mission, now attracting about a dozen to
Sunday services, continues to be supported by
Home Board language missions, through First
Church, Poplar.

On Wednesday nights an active program for
children draws 25-40 youngsters.

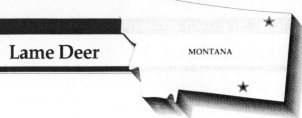

Morning Star Baptist Church

Mont. Rte. 39 & U.S. 212
Phone: 406/477-6264
Sunday Worship: 10:45 a.m.

IN 1964, A MISSIONARY COUPLE, Dick and Barbara Mefford, working among the Choctaws of Mississippi, was sent by the WMU of that state to serve a summer camp in Montana. Describing their work, the Meffords challenged Montana Southern Baptists to expand their Indian missions.

Montana Baptists in turn asked the Meffords to come help.

Two summers later, the Meffords had moved to Lame Deer.

Slowly they began winning the confidence of the Cheyennes, whose social customs and traditional religion "ran counter to the gospel." Converts were won as the Cheyennes, who called themselves the Morning Star People, were introduced to the One who is described in song as the "Bright and Morning Star."

The mission was constituted in 1980 as a church; it continues to be served by home missionaries.

Kooskia, Idaho

Clearwater Baptist Church
*Off Idaho Rte. 13, approx. 14 miles
  southeast of Kooskia*
Phone: 208/926-0811
Sunday Worship: 11 a.m.

THE FIRST SOUTHERN BAPTIST missionary in Idaho organized the Clearwater Church in 1887. Baptists from Arkansas and Oklahoma who had settled in the area then known as Independence Flat needed a church and called upon their former pastor and friend, Jacob Burrogh York. In September, the Baptist General Association of Western Arkansas and Indian Territory raised $234.50 to help send him as a minister to the Nez Perce Indians and early settlers.

York and his family left their Oklahoma home, journeyed by train to Raparia, Washington, by steamboat to Lewiston, then here by wagon. In December, shortly before organizing the church in a log schoolhouse, York reported back to the association that "this is a destitute field as far as Baptist preaching is concerned. I am the first Baptist preacher in this part of Idaho."

It was also reported the following year that one Sunday a bear "stampeded some of the Sunday school scholars" and regarding economic conditions that they could "raise anything on this side of Clearwater except money."

Circuit-riding until about age 74, York organized at least 18 other congregations in addition to caring for this church periodically for more than 20 years. After he resigned from Clearwater for the last time in 1909, the church became affiliated with Northern Baptists.

The church again became affiliated with Southern Baptists in 1981 when it was accepted into the Utah-Idaho convention.

Las Vegas, Nevada

First Baptist Church

300 South Ninth Street
Phone: 702/382-6177
Sunday Worship: 8:15 a.m.,
9:30 a.m. and 10:50 a.m.

PERHAPS THE FIRST BAPTIST church in the state was the congregation organized here by Homer Newberry of Michigan, although another church reputed to have been organized in Viriginia City (1873) may predate this one. Most of the early churches had difficulties surviving, especially in towns terrorized by the likes of "Billy the Kid."

In the early 1880s, only two Baptist churches had survived — the one in Virginia City and another at Reno. By 1885, the Las Vegas congregation was reestablished with its first permanent building, which was twice burned by arsonists.

Virginia City now has no Baptist church.

Redrock Baptist Church

5500 West Alta
Phone: 702/870-9198
Sunday Worship: 11 a.m. and 6:30 p.m.
Spanish Services: 7:30 p.m.

THE WEEK OF OCTOBER 15-21, 1978, was Southern Baptist Week in Nevada as 300 messengers gathered to organize the Nevada Area State Convention, forerunner of the present Southern Baptist state convention. They listed two priorities: strengthening churches and developing new congregations.

In conjunction with the constituting convention, the Baptist women organized the Woman's Missionary Union.

Started in 1955, the church is among the oldest Southern Baptist works in Las Vegas.

Roosevelt, Utah

Roosevelt Baptist Church
402 Hillcrest Drive
Phone: 801/722-3540
Sunday Worship: 11 a.m. and 7 p.m.

About 1918, a Baptist family moved from Texas to a farm near here. Without a Baptist church nearby, they attended a Congregational church and for a while sent their children to a Mormon Sunday School. The situation changed when in July, 1944, Rev. W. C. Bennett of Texas used the vacant Episcopal church building in which to hold revival services. With the group he gathered he organized the first Southern Baptist church in the state.

For the next two years the Roosevelt congregation met in the Episcopal facility until a Baptist sanctuary was completed. Now in its third building (1987), the church has been instrumental in starting much of the Southern Baptist work throughout the Utah-Idaho convention.

Ute Indian Baptist Church
1 mile north of U.S. 40 on White Rocks Road,
7 miles east of Roosevelt
Phone: 801/722-2389
Sunday Worship: 11 a.m. and 7 p.m.

The first Southern Baptist mission among the Ute Indians is located near the tribal headquarters at Ft. Duchesne, operating center of the Unitah-Ouray Reservation. The mission was begun in 1952 by the Roosevelt Church. In 1954, the Home Mission Board appointed a language missionary to help secure and continue the work; the mission has been supported by the Board and the Utah-Idaho convention since then.

In 1976, the mission organized as a church.

UTAH

First Southern Baptist Church
1175 West 6th North
Phone: 801/363-6094
Sunday Worship: 11:00 a.m. and 6:30 p.m.

ORGANIZED IN 1950 AS Rose Park Church by home missionary Ira Marks, the church bought land and built its current facilities 1951-1955. Its name was changed in 1963. Over the years, First Southern has sponsored six other churches and a Spanish work.

In 1964, the Utah-Idaho Southern Baptist Convention was organized here, by messengers from churches in the two-state area. Until then they were affiliated with the Arizona Southern Baptist Convention. For its first two years, Utah-Idaho convention offices were located in the upper story of the church.

First Baptist Church
777 South 13th Street
Phone: 801/582-4921
Sunday Worship: 11 a.m.

BAPTIST WORK IN UTAH BEGAN at Salt Lake City with the arrival in October, 1871, of Rev. Sewell Brown, appointed by the American Baptist Home Mission Society to spend half of his time between here and the Wyoming Territory. Although he gathered a congregation of about 20 people, little fruition came of his efforts due to much opposition from the Mormons. After only nine months he left, "shaking the dust from his feet at his departure."

The Baptist witness apparently remained silent until the supervisor of a mining company, a Baptist from Ohio, offered his house in 1883 for the first services of a Baptist congregation which became First Church. It is now affiliated with American Baptist Churches.

Other Sites of Interest

CORTEZ, COLORADO

First Southern Baptist Church *(300 North Elm)*. The oldest Southern Baptist Church in the state was organized in August, 1938, probably by L. H. Rischel, who had founded another church at Alamosa four years earlier. Both churches were affiliated with the New Mexico convention.

KIMBERLY, IDAHO

First Baptist Church *(Adams & Birch Streets)*. In 1950, a group meeting in homes decided to unite into a Southern Baptist church when none others existed in Idaho. Under the leadership of Rev. Alvin Bennet, they assembled at Grange Hall where they constituted and continued to meet for two years. Before 1953, on land previously owned by the Mormon Church, First Church constructed and moved into its own building.

LEWISTON, IDAHO

Orchards Baptist Church *(1002 Bryden Avenue)*. The first Southern Baptist church in northern Idaho was organized as the Clearwater Church in 1953, under the direction of area missionary Lewis Steed. A month later at Lewiston Orchards, from which the church adopted its present name, the congregation held a revival and on the last night voted to give 10 percent of its income to the Cooperative Program through the Oregon-Washington Baptist Convention. The church sponsored all of the early missions and churches in the Lewis-Clark Association, which remains affiliated with the Northwest Baptist Convention.

CROW AGENCY, MONTANA

Absaloka Baptist Church *(West of I-90)*. Jack and Linda Coward, catalytic missionaries appointed to the Billings region in 1980, worked with Indians on the Northern Cheyenne and Crow Reservations. By 1982, the Absaloka Church was constituted and located near the Crow Tribal headquarters, two miles northwest of Custer Battlefield National Monument.

HAWTHORNE, NEVADA

First Southern Baptist Church *(5th and C Streets)*.
Among the vast number of military personnel in the
state at the end of World War II were two Southern
Baptist deacons, Ben Felts and Lester Hampton. They
organized Babbitt Church at the naval base in 1947.
Initially independent, under their influence the church
affiliated with the Sacramento Valley Association in
California the following year. Thus began Southern
Baptist work in Nevada.

CRESCENT VALLEY, NEVADA

Crescent Valley Baptist Church *(Nev. Rte. 306, approx.
20 miles south of I-80)*. When this town of about 100
residents in northern Eureka County learned in 1963
that they would have a post office, 80-year-old "Doctor
John" Hawkins was there to get a postal box for a
Baptist church. The minister came out of retirement,
convinced of the growth potential and spiritual needs
of the town. He got help from local residents, including
those of other denominations, to help restore an old
house on property donated by the railroad company.

OGDEN, UTAH

First Baptist Church *(2519 Jefferson Street)*. The oldest
Baptist church in Utah was organized by American
Baptist home missionary Dwight Spencer in 1881. At
the time, no other Baptist church existed within 500
miles in any direction.

LARAMIE, WYOMING

First Baptist Church *(1517 Canby Street)*. The oldest
Baptist church in the state was organized by D. J.
Pierce, the first Baptist missionary to Wyoming
Territory, in 1870. The present sanctuary was built in
1908, following a fire which destroyed the original
building.

Pacific States

Missions on the Coastal Rim

THE PACIFIC COAST IS A LAND of discovery and diversity, a land of hope that draws people of every religion, race, age and economic status. The history of the region traces from the Spanish conquerers of the 1500s to the hundreds of settlers who followed the Oregon Trail in 1843.

Among them were a Missouri deacon and his wife. In their home near Portland, Oregon, was held the first Baptist services west of the Rockies.

But the real rush west, for Americans and for Baptists, began in 1848 when the discovery of gold in California spurred a tremendous influx. San Francisco became the major port through which prospecters and other travelers passed. Southern Baptist missionary Jehu Lewis Shuck sojourned there before sailing to China and witnessed to Chinese immigrants. He later returned to California as a home missionary.

Even before gold was discovered in 1896 further north, Baptists had found their way to Alaska. W.H.R. Corlies and his wife, Emily, came to Juneau in 1879, where in nearby Taku Harbor they gathered Indians for the first known Baptist worship services. A few years later two Baptist couples, in Kodiak as teachers, held prayer services. There, in 1893, Baptists established an orphanage, out of which grew Alaska's first Baptist church.

MIGRATION TO THE PACIFIC COAST didn't stop in the 19th century. The Depression, Dust Bowl and boll weevil brought refugees from southern states to California in the 1920s and 1930s. They planted churches, and in 1941 the Southern Baptist General Convention of California held its first meeting.

The state's population has practically doubled in

the past three decades, and California Southern Baptists have grown to almost 400,000 in 1,400 congregations. They work in more than 40 languages and among some 70 cultures. The first Baptist missions among Chinese, Filipinos, Lahu and Vietnamese were recorded here.

In the 1940s shipyards and related wartime industries brought new residents, including more Baptists from the South, to the North Pacific Coast. Additional churches and outreach were needed. An aggressive missions program was organized in 1942, and two years later Southern Baptists formed the Northwest Association. In 1953 a church in British Columbia was the first of several Canadian churches to seek affiliation with the new convention. Churches were planted not only in Oregon and Washington, but in northern Idaho and three provinces of Canada. From the convention office in Portland to its most distant church in Manitoba was about 2,500 miles.

Alaska saw another influx of settlers with the discovery of black gold — oil — in 1957. The Alaska Baptist convention, organized in 1946, has continued to grow.

Southern Baptists came to Hawaii from the Orient: In 1937, when political conflicts were escalating into war, foreign missionaries began retreating there from China, Korea and Japan. Finding that

Southern Baptist work had already been started by a local businessman, missionaries supported his effort. As a result, several churches were started by 1943 and an association was formed.

Hawaii is a crossroads in the Pacific, a stopping ground for many traveling East or West. Every major religion in the world, particularly those of the Orient, is represented on the islands.

With the economic base of international trade shifting from the Atlantic to the Pacific, Hawaii and other Pacific Rim states are apt to become even more a focal point in world trade and culture.

They are likely to become a focal point for world evangelism, too, as Southern Baptists move into the 21st century.

The first Baptist church in California to affiliate with Southern Baptists was in Shafter.

FIRST SOUTHERN+
+BAPTIST CHURCH

Hillsboro, Oregon

OREGON

West Union Church
West Union Road, 1 mile north of U.S. 26,
approx. 3/4 mile west of Cornelius Road
Phone: 503/649-2510
Sunday Worship: 9:30 a.m.

THE FIRST BAPTIST MISSION in the Northwest was begun as a "lay movement." A Missouri couple, David and Louisa Lenox, held worship services as they migrated west on the Oregon Trail. Upon arrival in 1843, they opened their log home for regular worship and prayer services. The following spring they organized into a Baptist church — the first west of the Rockies, the next closest 2,000 miles away.

First Baptist Church, Klamath Falls
707 High Street
Phone: 503/884-6274
Sunday worship: 11 a.m. and 6 p.m.

THE OLDEST CHURCH AFFILIATED with the Northwest Baptist Convention was founded in 1884 and pastored until 1910 by J.B. Griffith of Georgia. During that period, the church aligned with the Baptist Convention of the North Pacific Coast, a group of Baptists whose repeated efforts to affiliate with the SBC were denied, to respect comity agreements with Northern Baptists. Even knowing that the southern agency could not send missionaries, Northwest Baptists still sent money to the Home Mission Board. Due to meager resources, the young convention dissolved in 1900.

The church had various affiliations until calling as pastor Southern Baptist Leonard B. Sigel, one of the Northwest's great church starters. Klamath Falls, with other churches, organized the Northwest Convention in 1948.

Los Angeles, California

Berendo Street Church
975 South Berendo Street
Phone: 213/383-4982
Sunday Worship: 11 a.m.

U PON EARNING DEGREES at Southwestern Seminary in 1957, Don and Eisook Kim were appointed by the Home Mission Board to minister to Korean and other international students in Los Angeles. Begun only a year after the first Korean Baptist church in America was constituted (in Washington, D.C.), Berendo Street became the first Baptist mission among Koreans on the West Coast.

Fourteen years later, only three Korean churches existed nationwide. Now nearly 300 Korean Southern Baptist churches are located among more than 30 states and American Samoa.

First Filipino Church
837 South Park View
Phone: 213/254-6669
Sunday Worship: 11 a.m.

B APTIST WORK AMONG Filipinos in America began in California. Southern Baptists started their work when Filipinos who were part of the Emmanuel Church organized in Fresno in 1961.

The first Filipino Southern Baptist congregation, however, came about when Eduardo Peol, former host of the "Baptist Hour" in the Phillippines, immigrated to the U.S. in 1964 to attend Golden Gate Baptist seminary. After launching three Bible studies, he started Sunday morning worship services at the Filipino-American Center and evening services at the Bamboo Grove Restaurant. Appointed as a missionary by the Home Mission Board, Peol used an HMB church loan to purchase this site from First Southern Baptist Church in 1972. First Filipino constituted two years later.

Sacramento

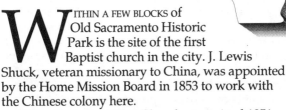

First Baptist Church
4th Street,
between K and L Streets
Phone: 916/443-6537
Sunday Worship: 8:30 am.
and 10:50 a.m.

CALIFORNIA

WITHIN A FEW BLOCKS of Old Sacramento Historic Park is the site of the first Baptist church in the city. J. Lewis Shuck, veteran missionary to China, was appointed by the Home Mission Board in 1853 to work with the Chinese colony here.

When he arrived First Church, organized 1851, was pastorless. So in addition to starting the first Chinese Baptist church in America, he pastored the Anglo church and helped Blacks to start their own church in 1857.

While here, Shuck baptized about 60 persons "representing Europe, Asia, Africa, and both North and Central America."

Financial stringencies and approaching war interrupted the Southern Baptist mission work.

First Chinese Church site
6th Street, between G and H Streets

IN 1855, A CHAPEL FOR THE first Chinese Baptist congregation in America was founded by Shuck, assisted by Chinese lay preachers Ah Mooey and Ah (Leong) Chak. Shuck reported that these two "speak regularly . . . and boldly avow their faith in Christ before their countrymen." After Shuck resigned in 1859, the two Chinese Baptists were appointed by the Foreign Mission Board to Canton, China.

San Francisco, California

CALIFORNIA

First Baptist Church
21 Octavia Street at Market Street
Phone: 415/863-3382
Sunday Worship: 10:45 a.m. and 7 p.m.

ABOUT THE TIME that Southern Baptist missionary J. Lewis Shuck sailed for China, after spending some months working in San Francisco, O. C. Wheeler arrived here as a misssionary appointed by Northern Baptists. Within four months, Wheeler organized on July 6, 1849, the first Baptist church in California. By the following year Wheeler took note of 46 Baptist preachers who passed through San Francisco on their way to the mining camps.

By 1851, one year after statehood, three Baptist churches had been established in the state. Together they organized the San Francisco Association and voted to correspond with the American Baptist Home Mission Society and the Southern Baptist Convention.

With a rapidly expanding population during the Gold Rush, the association identified 25 potential fields of work needing missionaries. In response to their correspondence, the Domestic (Home) Mission Board recommended to the Southern Convention that missionaries be sent, and the next year appointed Shuck to work in California.

That work didn't last, and First Church affiliated with Northern Baptists until recently when, true to its heritage, the church re-joined the Southern Baptist Convention.

Today it is a dually aligned congregation, just as it was more than a century ago.

Shafter, California

First Southern Baptist Church
250 North Kern Street
Phone: 805/746-6774
Sunday Worship: 10:45 a.m. and 6 p.m.

TEXANS, OKLAHOMANS AND ARKANSANS left destitute by the Depression and the Dust Bowl of the 1930s relocated with new hopes to the Pacific coastal states. When preaching a revival at Shafter, R. W. Lackey (later to become first Executive Director of the California Southern Baptist Convention) found that 123 of 126 people in attendance were "Okies." Many of these transplanted residents were Southern Baptists who were uncomfortable without the familiar worship they had known.

A group in Shaster organized its own congregation on May 10, 1936, known as the Independent Orthodox Missionary Baptist Church, which became the first constituted church in the new era of California Southern Baptists. A woman's auxiliary also was organized here in 1938, which was the first Southern Baptist church WMU in the state.

At this church in 1940 12 other churches met to form the Southern Baptist General Convention of California.

Two years later, the new state convention was recognized by the Southern Baptist Convention — but by only a narrow margin of votes. Those opposing its recognition emphasized "respect [for] agreements with other Baptist bodies" regarding territorial limits. Questions were even raised about the ability to judge the doctrinal integrity of churches so distant from the southern states, that California Baptists might be outside the mainstream of Southern Baptist thought and practice.

Those in favor of the new state convention, however, won with their appeal that the 1845 purpose of the convention was to "provide a general organization for Baptists in the United States and its territories."

Anchorage, Alaska

First Baptist Church
1100 West 10th Avenue
Phone: 901/279-8481
Sunday Worship: 11 a.m. and 6 p.m.

THE FIRST SOUTHERN BAPTIST CHURCH in Alaska had its beginnings in the Church of the Open Door. There two Southern Baptist chaplains, Aubrey Halsell and Jewell D. Foster, preached a revival service in September 1943, which resulted in 22 conversions and the constitution of First Church.

Within a few months, the new congregation renovated a fire-gutted house on Sixth Street which was purchased from "the madam of a bawdy house."

The first civilian pastor, William Petty, began publishing *The Alaska Baptist Messenger*. The next pastor was Felton Griffin (1945- 73), who served as president, vice-president and executive secretary of the Alaska Baptist Convention. He was instrumental in affiliating Alaska churches with the Southern Baptist Convention.

First Church, which has sponsored several missions, is now in its third building.

Baptist Native School of Theology
East Third Baptist Church
802 East Third Avenue
Phone: 907/277-3985
Sunday Worship: 11 a.m. and 7 p.m.

BEGUN IN 1957 TO PROVIDE TRAINING for Native ministers, Alaska Baptist School's first graduates were Willie and Martha Johnson, the first Eskimos appointed by the Home Mission Board. Shortly thereafter the school closed but was reopened in 1978 in the facilities of East Third Baptist, co-sponsored by the Alaska Baptist Convention and the Home Mission Board.

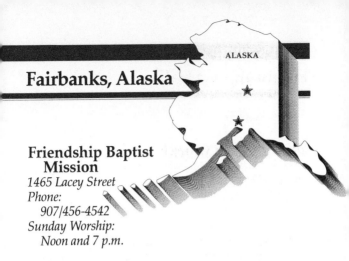

Fairbanks, Alaska

ALASKA

Friendship Baptist Mission
1465 Lacey Street
Phone:
  907/456-4542
Sunday Worship:
  Noon and 7 p.m.

BEGUN IN 1947, THE MISSION acquired this property three years later and then deeded it to the Home Mission Board. Here in August, 1953, was constituted the first Southern Baptist church for Alaska Natives.

The congregation in turn sponsored Native missions in Kotzebue and Nenana and what is now the Shannon Park Church.

Native Baptist Church, Friendship's original congregation, reverted to mission status in 1955. The name changed to Friendship during the 12-year tenure of home missionaries John and Lillian Isaacs, who established literacy missions and expanded the work to serve Internationals as well as Natives.

Their exemplary pilot program in literacy, English-as-a-Second language and citizenship for Internationals has been expanded to an English/ Citizenship school, and that and the mission's other programs continue to be directed by home missionaries.

Honolulu, Hawaii

Olivet Baptist Church
1775 South Beretania Street
Phone: 808/946-6505
Sunday Worship: 10:45 a.m. and 7 p.m.

ORGANIZED IN 1941 AS A RESULT of a mission begun by a Christian lawyer in 1926, Olivet became the mother church for many other Southern Baptist congregations in Hawaii.

It was a mission of First Baptist Church *(1313 Pensacola Street)*, which was organized in 1930 in the Kuhio School on King Street, the first Baptist church in Hawaii. Known then as Calvary Church, it was soon followed by the establishment of four other churches—Nuuanu and Olivet in Honolulu, Wahiawa further north on Oahu, and Waimea on Kauai.

In 1943, five years after mission work had been started in the Territory by the Foreign Mission Board, these five churches met at Calvary (now First) to form an association which was the beginning of the Hawaii Baptist Convention. Committees were established for missions and evangelism, Brotherhood and WMU. Maude B. Dozier became president and Sue Saito Nishikawa was executive secretary.

Shortly thereafter Calvary, however, disassociated itself from the convention and took the name First Church. It is presently affiliated with American Baptist Churches. The other four of the first Hawaii Baptist churches have remained aligned with Southern Baptists.

Today Olivet is a multi-national congregation with members who are of Anglo, Black, Japanese, Korean, Chinese and Filipino descent.

First Baptist Church
1233 California Avenue
Phone: 808/622-4321
Sunday Worship: 10:40 a.m. and 7 p.m.

IN 1820 CONGREGATIONAL MISSIONARIES came to the islands. But not until 1926 did Baptist work begin. Rev. Charles J. McDonald, a Honolulu businessman, started a Sunday School in a nearby playground pavilion. By 1934, there were enough converts with interest to constitute a church. It was the plea of Rev. McDonald that eventuated the decision of the Foreign Mission Board to "lend" personnel to the territory, and thereby began expanding the work of Southern Baptists across the islands.

This work was greatly boosted when, in 1945, 17 young people of the Wahiawa church dedicated their lives to pastoral or full- time ministries. One of these, Samuel Choy, after serving as a missionary to Korea, became Hawaii Baptists' first director of missions.

This is the oldest Southern Baptist church in Hawaii.

Rev. McDonald had earlier started First Baptist Church in Honolulu.

Other Sites of Interest

KOTZEBUE, ALASKA

First Baptist Church. Here in one of the largest Eskimo villages, where the summer sun does not set for 36 consecutive days, is located the northernmost Southern Baptist church. Catalytic missionary Harley Shield travels by bush plane to surrounding villages, while Mission Service Corps volunteers provide leadership at First Church. Inland, at Kobuk, Southern Baptists held the first baptism by any denomination north of the Arctic Circle.

BUENA PARK, CALIFORNIA

Knott's Berry Farm *(8039 Beach Boulevard)*. In the Old West section of this popular amusement park is the first meeting house which served the Baptist Church of Downey, organized in 1868 mostly by Southerners. One of its pastors, James Edward Barnes, a Kentucky native who had come here to pan for gold, preached on Sundays while mining on weekdays. After Southern Baptist mission work ceased in California, Barnes was the only delegate from California to the Southern Convention. As an evangelist and pastor among southern California churches, he was a "lone voice in the wilderness" speaking out on behalf of Southern Baptists.

SAN DIEGO, CALIFORNIA

El Cajon Vietnamese Mission *(660 South Third Street)*, the first Vietnamese Southern Baptist congregation, was organized here in June, 1975, shortly after SBC churches began resettling refugees from Vietnam. Sponsored by Meridian Southern Baptist Church, the church has been pastored by home missionary Bingh T. Phan since it began. By 1985, more than 90 Vietnamese Southern Baptist congregations existed in the U.S. — more than had been started in Vietnam.

SAN FRANCISCO, CALIFORNIA

First Chinese Southern Church *(1255 Hyde Street)*, was Southern Baptists' first Chinese congregation after they re-entered California in the 1940s. Organized in 1955 by Peter Chen, a native of Shanghai, China, and home missionary, the church is situated on the edge of the city's famous Chinatown. While pastoring here, Chen helped found and then pastored the Grace Chinese Baptist Church.

SANTA ROSA, CALIFORNIA
Community Church (*1228 Grand Avenue*). In the late 19th century, Black Baptists formed separate national conventions. For the next half-century relatively few Blacks attended White Southern Baptist churches. In 1951, Community Church became the first all-Black congregation to cooperate with the SBC. By 1980, about 600 Black churches were affiliated with the SBC.

HILO, HAWAII
Kinoole Church (*1815 Kinoole Street*), is first Southern Baptist church and "mother church" to all others on the Big Island. The church was organized in 1946, the same year a major tidal wave hit the area. Salvaged lumber was used to build the meeting house in which the church gathers today.

PORTLAND, OREGON
First Church of the Deaf (*2003 SE Larch*), in 1975, became the first independent deaf church in the Southern Baptist Convention. A decade later, more than 800 deaf congregations or units of work existed in the SBC.

WARM SPRINGS, OREGON
Warm Springs Church (*U.S. 26, approx. 14 miles northwest of Madras*). In 1958, a Southern Baptist mission was established by Edward Branch near Warm Springs Reservation, where live the confederated tribes of Warm Springs, Wishram and Paiute Indians. About that time, Allen Elston, after reading the home mission book, *The Tribes Go Up*, dedicated his life to Indian missions. Since his appointment by the Home Mission Board in 1960, Elston has worked at this site. The Warm Springs congregation, now meeting on the reservation, constituted as a church in 1969.

LONGVIEW, WASHINGTON
First Baptist Church (*1718 East Kessler Boulevard*). Organized in 1937 by Leonard. B. Sigle (1905-1975), this was the first Southern Baptist church in the state. Sigle, during his 40 years of pastoral ministry, planted more than 40 churches; he was also founding editor of the *Pacific Coast Baptist* (now *Northwest Baptist*), which gave voice to a movement to organize Southern Baptists into an Oregon-Washington state convention.

For More Information

To learn more about historical sites, places to visit and the work of Southern Baptists in each state:

Alabama Baptist State Convention
3310 Independence Drive
Montgomery, AL 36198 • (205) 288-2460

Alaska Baptist Convention
1750 O'Malley Road
Anchorage, AK 99516-1371 • (907) 344-9627

Arizona Southern Baptist Convention
400 West Camelback Road
Phoenix, AZ 85013 • (602) 264-9421

Arkansas Baptist State Convention
525 West Capitol
Little Rock, AR 72203 • (501) 376-4791

California Southern Baptist Convention
678 East Shaw Avenue
Fresno, CA 93710 • (209) 229-9533

Colorado Baptist General Convention
7393 South Alton Way
Englewood, CO 80112-2372 • (303) 771-2480

Dakota Fellowship of Southern Baptist Churches
4007 North State Street
Bismarck, ND 58501 • (701) 255-3765

District of Columbia Baptist Convention
1628 Sixteenth St, NW
Washington, DC 20009 • (202) 265-1526

Florida Baptist Convention
1230 Hendricks Avenue
Jacksonville, FL 32207 • (904) 396-2351

Georgia, Baptist Convention of
2930 Flowers Road SE
Atlanta, GA 30341 • (404) 455-0404

Hawaii Baptist Convention
2042 Vancouver Drive
Honolulu, HI 96822 • (808) 946-9581

Illinois Baptist State Association
3085 Stevenson Drive
Springfield, IL 62794-9247 • (217) 786-2600

Indiana, State Convention of Baptists in
900 North High School Road
Indianapolis, IN 46224 • (317) 241-9317

Iowa Southern Baptist Fellowship
2400 Eighty-Sixth Street, #27
Des Moines, IA 50322 • (515) 278-1566

Kansas-Nebraska Convention of Southern Baptists
5410 West Seventh Street
Topeka, KS 66606-2398 913 273-4880

Kentucky Baptist Convention
10701 Shelbyville Road
Middletown, KY 40241 • (502) 245-4101

Louisiana Baptist Convention
1250 MacArthur Drive
Alexandria, LA 71309 • (318) 448-3402

Maryland/Delaware, Baptist Convention of
1313 York Road
Lutherville, MD 21093 • (301) 321-7900

Michigan, Baptist State Convention of
15635 West Twelve Mile Road
Southfield, MI 48076 • (313) 557-4200

Minnesota-Wisconsin Southern Baptist Convention
519 Sixteenth Street, SE
Rochester, MN 55904 • (507) 282-3636

Mississippi Baptist Convention
515 Mississippi Street
Jackson, MS 39205 • (601) 968-3800

Missouri Baptist Convention
400 East High Street
Jefferson City, MO 65101 • (314) 635-7931

Montana Southern Baptist Fellowship
332 Grand Avenue
Billings, MT 59101 • (406) 252-7537

Nevada Baptist Convention
406 California Avenue
Reno, NV 89509-1520 • (702) 786-0406

New England, Baptist Convention of
5 Oak Avenue
Northborough, MA 01532 • (508) 393-6013

New Mexico, Baptist Convention of
616 Central Aveune, SE
Albuquerque, NM 87103 • (505) 247-0586

Information

New York, Baptist Convention of
6538 Collamer Rd East
Syracuse, NY 13057 • (315) 433-1001

North Carolina, Baptist State Convention of
205 Convention Dr.
Cary, NC 27511-1107 • (919) 467-5100

Northwest Baptist Convention
1033 N.E. 6th Avenue
Portland, OR 97232 • (503) 238-4545

Ohio, State Convention of Baptists in
1680 East Broad
Columbus, OH 43203 • (614) 258-8491

Oklahoma, Baptist General Convention of
1141 North Robinson
Oklahoma City, OK 73103 • (405) 236-4341

Pennsylvania-South Jersey, Baptist Convention of
4620 Fritchey Street
Harrisburg, PA 17109-2895 • (717) 652-5856

South Carolina Baptist Convention
907 Richland Street
Columbia, SC 29201 • (803) 765-0030

Tennessee Baptist Convention
205 Franklin Pike
Brentwood, TN 37024-0728 • (615) 373-2255

Texas, Baptist General Convention of
333 North Washington
Dallas, TX 75426-1798 • (214) 828-5100

Utah-Idaho Southern Baptist Convention
8649 South 1300 East
Sandy, UT 84091 • (801) 255-3565

Virginia, Baptist General Association of
2828 Emerywood Parkway
Richmond, VA 23226 • (804) 282-9751

West Virginia Convention of Southern Baptists
801 Sixth Avenue
St. Albans, WV 25177 • (304) 727-2974

Wyoming Southern Baptist Convention
318 West B Street
Casper, WY 82602 • (307) 472-4087

For Further Reading

Allen, Catherine. *A Century to Celebrate: History of the Woman's Missionary Union.* Birmingham: Woman's Missionary Union, 1987.
————. *Laborers Together for God: 22 Great Women in Baptist Life.* Birmingham: Woman's Missionary Union, 1987.

Baker, Robert A. *A Baptist Source Book, with Particular Reference to Southern Baptists.* Nashville: Broadman Press, 1966.
————. *The Southern Baptist Convention and Its People, 1607-1902.* Nashville: Broadman, 1974.

Baptist History and Heritage. [periodical]. Nashville: Historical Commission, 1965- .

Barnes, William Wright. *The Southern Baptist Convention, 1845-1953.* Nashville: Broadman, 1954.

Belvin, B. Frank. *The Tribes Go Up: A Study of the American Indian.* Atlanta: Home Mission Board, 1955.

Burton, Joe W. *Road to Augusta: R.B.C. Howell and the Formation of the Southern Baptist Convention.* Nashville: Broadman, 1976.
————. *Road to Recovery: Southern Baptist Renewal Following the Civil War, as seen especially in the Work of I.T. Tichenor.* Nashville: Broadman, 1977.

Cauthen, Baker J., et al. *Advance: A History of Southern Baptist Foreign Missions.* Nashville: Broadman, 1981.

Encyclopedia of Southern Baptists, 4 vols. Nashville: Broadman, 1958-1982.

McBeth, H. Leon. *The Baptist Heritage.* Nashville: Broadman, 1987.
————. *Women in Baptist Life.* Nashville: Broadman, 1979.

Rutledge, Arthur B. and William G. Tanner. *Mission to America: A History of Southern Baptist Home Missions.* (2nd rev. ed.). Nashville: Broadman, 1983.

Sorrill, Bobbie. *Annie Armstrong: Dreamer in Action.* Nashville: Broadman, 1984.

■ DEDICATION

To Wendell Belew . . . *long-time friend of the WMU, and a modern-day Luther Rice, who for 30 years has travelled miles for missions, inspiring men and women with his dreams of how far the Kingdom stretches when Baptists cooperate in missions.*

And to Larry Lewis, president of the Home Mission Board, whose insight and interest have made this book possible.

■ ACKNOWLEDGMENTS

The following people gave valuable help in gathering this material:

From the Home Mission Board: Wendell Belew, E.W. Hunke Jr., Ernest J. Kelley

From the Woman's Missionary Union: Eljee Bentley

EDITING AND DESIGN: Everett Hullum

Additional editing: Tom Peterson

Coursey, W. Tony
  A Baptist Journey.

Bibliography: p. 128
1. Baptists—U.S.—History. 2. Churches, Baptists—Guide-books.
3. United States—Description and travel—Guide-books. 4. United States—Religious and ecclesiastical institutions, etc. 5. Historic Sites—U.S.—Guide books. I. Title. II. Title: A Travel Guide to Baptist Historic Sites in the U.S.   BX 6235.C69 1989   286/.173

ISBN 0-936625-75-9 (pbk.)
Library of Congress Catalog Card Number: 89-051051